Slavery in the Americas: *African Americans during the Civil War*

Copyright © 2006 by Infobase Publishing

Chelsea House
An imprint of Infobase Publishing
132 West 31st Street
New York NY 10001

Library of Congress Cataloging-in-Publication Data
DeFord, Deborah H.
    African Americans during the Civil War / Deborah H. DeFord.
          p. cm. —(Slavery in the Americas)
    Includes bibliographical references and index.
    ISBN 0-8160-6138-6
    1. United States—History—Civil War, 1861–1865—Participation, African American—Juvenile literature.
    2. United States Army—African American troops—History—19th century—Juvenile literature.
    3. African American soldiers—History—19th century—Juvenile literature. I. Title. II. Series.
    E540.N3D44 2006
    973.7'415—dc22

                          2005021497

Cover design by Smart Graphics
A Creative Media Applications Production
Interior design: Fabia Wargin & Luís Leon
Editor: Matt Levine
Copy editor: Laurie Lieb
Proofreader: Tania Bissell
Photo researcher: Jennifer Bright

Photo Credits:
Associated Press pages: title page, 10, 18, 26, 90, 104, 105, 106; The Granger Collection pages: 5, 43, 49, 58, 74, 77, 86, 89, 97, 100; Picture History page: 17; New York Public Library, Astor, Lenox and Tilden Foundations pages: 24, 31, 33, 39, 41, 45, 51, 55, 56, 61, 65, 87, 93; Getty Images pages: 67, 71

Printed in the United States of America

VB PKG 10 9 8 7 6 5 4 3 2 1

PREVIOUS PAGE:

A band of African-American troops poses for a photo during the Civil War. Free blacks, as well as escaped slaves, fought bravely in the war to end slaves' captivity.

Contents

Preface to the Series

Philip Schwarz, Ph.D., *General Editor*

In order to understand American history, it is essential to know that for nearly two centuries, Americans in the 13 colonies and then in the United States bought imported Africans and kept them and their descendants in bondage. In his second inaugural address in March 1865, President Abraham Lincoln mentioned the "250 years of unrequited toil" that slaves had endured in America. Slavery lasted so long and controlled so many people's lives that it may seem impossible to comprehend the phenomenon and to know the people involved. Yet it is extremely difficult to grasp many aspects of life in today's United States without learning about slavery's role in the lives and development of the American people.

Slavery probably existed before history began to be recorded, but the first known dates of slavery are about 1600 B.C. in Greece and as early as 2700 B.C. in Mesopotamia (present-day Iraq). Although there are institutions that resemble slavery in some modern societies, slavery in its actual sense is illegal everywhere. Yet historical slavery still affects today's free societies.

Numerous ancient and modern slave societies were based on chattel slavery—the legal ownership of human beings, not just their labor. The Bible's Old and New Testaments, as well as other ancient historical documents, describe enslaved people. Throughout history, there were slaves in African, Middle Eastern, South Asian, and East Asian societies, as well as in the Americas—and of course, there were slaves in European countries. (One origin of the word *slave* is the medieval Latin *sclavus,* which not only means "slave" but also "Slav." The Slavs were people of eastern Europe who were conquered in the 800s and often sold as slaves.)

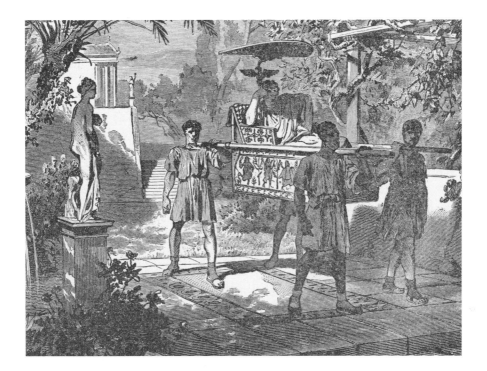

This drawing shows slaves carrying their master in a garden in ancient Rome. Slaves were a part of many societies from ancient times until the mid-1800s.

People found as many excuses or justifications for enslaving other people as there were slaveholding societies. Members of one ethnic group claimed that cultural differences justified enslaving people of another group. People with long histories of conflict with other groups might conclude that those other people were inferior in some cultural way. Citizens of ancient Greece and Rome, among others, claimed they could hold other people in bondage because these people were "barbarians" or prisoners of war. Racism played a major part in European decisions to enslave Africans. European colonists in the Americas commonly argued that Africans and their descendants were naturally inferior to Europeans, so it was morally acceptable to enslave them.

New World slavery deeply affected both Africa and the Americas. African society changed dramatically when the Atlantic slave trade began to carry so many Africans away. Some African societies were weakened by the regular buying or kidnapping of valued community members.

Western Hemisphere societies also underwent extraordinary changes when slavery of Africans was established there. Black slavery in North America was part of society from the earliest colonial settlements until the end of the U.S. Civil War. Many people consider the sale of about 20 Africans in Jamestown, Virginia, in 1619 the beginning of African slavery in what became the United States. American Indians and, later, Africans also were enslaved in Spanish colonies such as today's Florida and California and the islands of the Caribbean.

In early to mid-17th-century colonial North America, slavery developed slowly, beginning in Maryland and Virginia and spreading to the Carolinas in the 1670s. Southern colonists originally relied on white European servants. However, many of these servants had signed contracts to work only for a certain number of years, often to pay for their passage to North America. They became free when these contracts expired. Other servants rebelled or escaped. When fewer Europeans were available as servants, the servants' prices rose. The colonists hoped to find a more easily controlled and cheaper labor supply. European slave traders captured and imported more Africans, and slave prices dropped.

Soon, American plantations became strong markets for enslaved Africans. Tobacco plantation owners in the colonies around Chesapeake Bay—Maryland, Virginia, and North Carolina—and rice growers in South Carolina pressured slave traders to supply more slaves. In time, more and more slaves were kidnapped from their homes in Africa and taken to the colonies in chains to cultivate crops on the growing number of Southern plantations. Slaves were also taken to the Northern colonies to be farm workers, household servants, and artisans. In 1790, the U.S. enslaved population was less than 700,000. By 1860, it had risen to 3,953,750.

Similar circumstances transformed the Caribbean and South American societies and economies into plantation economies. There was a high demand for sugar in Europe, so British, French, Spanish, Portuguese, and other European colonists tried to fill that need. Brazil, a Portuguese colony, also became a thriving coffee-producing region. As the sugar and coffee planters became successful, they increased the size of their plantations and therefore needed more slaves to do the work. By 1790, Brazil was the largest American colonial slave society—that is, a society whose economy and social structure were grounded in slavery. Some 1,442,800 enslaved people lived in Brazil in 1790—twice the number that lived in the United States. Brazil's slave population grew slowly, however; in 1860, it was still only about 1,715,000. However, South American slaves were forced to work extremely hard in the tropical heat. The death rate of Caribbean and South American plantation workers was much higher than that of the North American slaves. Occasionally, a North American slave owner would threaten to sell unruly slaves to the West Indies or South America. Enslaved people took the threat seriously because the West Indies' bad reputation was widespread.

It is estimated that at least 11.8 million people were captured and shipped from Africa to the Americas. Many died during the slave ship voyage across the Atlantic Ocean. About 10 million survived and were sold in the Americas from 1519 to 1867. Nearly one-third of those people went to Brazil, while only about 3.8 percent (391,000) came to North America.

If the 1619 "first Africans" were slaves—the record is not completely clear—then there was a massive increase of the enslaved North American population from 20 or so people to nearly 4 million. In 1860, known descendants of Africans, both enslaved and free, numbered approximately 4.5 million, or about 14 percent of the U.S. population.

Slaveholders thought several numbers best measured their social, political, and economic status. These were the number of human beings they owned, the money and labor value of those people, and the proportion of slaveholders' total investment in human beings. By the 1800s, Southern slaveholders usually held two-thirds of their worth in human property. The largest slave owners were normally the wealthiest people in their area. For example, one Virginian colonist, Robert "King" Carter, who died in 1733, owned 734 slaves.

Consider what it took for slavery to begin in North America and to last all the way to 1865 in the South. This historical phenomenon did not "just occur." Both slave owning and enslaved people made many decisions concerning enslavement.

Should people hold other people in lifetime bondage? Could Africans be imported without damaging American colonial societies? Should colonists give up slavery? It took many years before Americans reached consensus on these subjects. White people's consensus in the North eventually led to the outlawing of slavery there. The Southern white consensus was clearly proslavery. Enslaved peoples had to make different decisions. Should slaves resist slavery individually or in groups? Should they raise families when their children were likely to live and die in bondage? Over the two centuries in which North American slavery existed, enslaved people changed their opinions concerning these questions.

Some white colonists initially tried to own Indian slaves. However, because the Indians knew the local environment, they could escape somewhat easily, especially because their free relatives and friends would try to protect them. Also, European diseases simply killed many of these Indians. Once European enslavement of American Indians died out in the 18th century, Africans and their African-American descendants were the only slaves in America. The Africans and their children were people with a history. They represented numerous African societies from West Africa to Madagascar in the western Indian Ocean. They endured and survived, creating their own American history.

When Africans began families in North America, they created a new genealogy and new traditions regarding how to survive as slaves. They agonized over such matters as violent, or even group, resistance—if it was unlikely to succeed, why try? By the 1800s, they endured family losses to the interstate slave trade. Black families suffered new separations that often were as wrenching as those caused by the journey from Africa. Large numbers of black Americans were forced to move from the older (Upper South) states to the newer (Deep South) territories and states. They were often ripped from their families and everything they knew and forced to live and work in faraway places.

This undated illustration of pre–Civil War life depicts African men being held in slave pens in Washington, D.C., about 1850.

There was only so much that African-American people could do to resist enslavement once it became well established in America. People sometimes ask why slaves did not try to end their bondage by revolting. Some did, but they rarely succeeded in freeing themselves. Most individual "revolts"—more accurately termed resistance—were very localized and were more likely to succeed than large-scale revolts. A man or woman might refuse to do what owners wanted, take the punishment, and find another way to resist. Some were so effective in day-to-day resistance that they can be called successful. Others failed and then decided that they had to try to find ways to survive slavery and enjoy some aspects of life. Those who escaped as "fugitives," temporarily or permanently, were the most successful resisters. Frederick Douglass and Harriet Tubman are the most famous escapees. Solomon Northup was unique: He was born free, then kidnapped and sold into slavery. Northup escaped and published his story.

Although inhumane and designed to benefit slave owners, slavery was a very "human" institution. That is, slaveholders and enslaved people interacted in many different ways. The stories of individuals reveal this frequently complex human interaction.

There were, for example, in all the Southern states, free African Americans who became slave owners. They protected their own family members from slavery, but owned other human beings for profit. One such black slave owner, William Johnson of Mississippi, controlled his human property using the same techniques, both mild and harsh, as did white slave owners. Robert Lumpkin, a slave trader from Richmond, Virginia, sold thousands of human beings to

Deep South buyers. Yet Lumpkin had a formerly enslaved wife to whom he willed all his Virginia, Alabama, and Pennsylvania property in 1866. Lumpkin sent their children to Massachusetts and Pennsylvania for their education and protection. He also freed other slaves before 1865. How could men such as these justify protecting their own families, but at the same time separating so many other families?

The Thirteenth Amendment ended slavery in the United States. However, former slaves were often kept from owning property and did not share the same rights as white Americans. Racist laws and practices kept the status of black Americans low. Even though slavery ended well over a century ago, the descendants of slave owners and of slaves are still generally on markedly different economic levels from each other.

The Civil War and Reconstruction created massive upheaval in Southern slave and free black communities. In addition, slave owners were often devastated. African Americans were "free at last," but their freedom was not guaranteed. A century passed before their legal rights were effectively protected and their political participation expanded. The Reverend Martin Luther King's "I have a dream" speech placed the struggle in historical context: He said he had a dream that "the sons of former slaves and the sons of former slave owners will be able to sit down together at the table of brotherhood." (Today, he would surely mention daughters as well.) The weight of history had already delayed that dream's coming to pass and can still do so. Knowing the history of slavery and emancipation will help fulfill the dream.

Introduction

In the Civil War, victory for the Union would mean freedom for all the slaves in the South. African Americans wanted the chance to help fight for that victory.

By 1861, when the Civil War (1861–1865) began in the United States, slavery still existed only in the South. All of the Northern states had outlawed slavery by 1850.

Just months before the start of the Civil War, seven Southern states decided to secede, or leave the United States. They wanted to protect their right to decide on the lawfulness of slavery. They also wanted to be able to carry slavery into the new Western territories that were opening up across North America. Meanwhile, many Northerners opposed slavery. The U.S. government had begun to pass laws that would limit and eventually prohibit slavery.

The most vocal Northerners opposed to slavery were the abolitionists, both black and white. They believed that slavery should be ended everywhere right away. Other Northerners believed that slavery was evil, but for the sake of peace, slaveholders should be allowed to keep the slaves they had. Still others did not want the slaves to be freed for fear that the freed people would move North and take their jobs.

In the South, most whites held racist views that made it possible for them to justify slavery. They claimed that African Americans were inferior to white people and were better off as slaves than if they were free. These whites also believed that if the millions of slaves were freed, they would violently turn against their former owners.

THE ROAD TO WAR

In 1850, U.S. legislators attempted to resolve the argument over slavery by passing a set of laws called the Compromise of 1850. The compromise declared certain new regions "free" and certain others "slave." It also included the Fugitive Slave Act of 1850. This law stated that it was illegal to help slaves escape or to interfere with their recapture, no matter how long ago they had escaped to the North. It also denied slaves the right to a trial by jury. Instead, government-appointed commissioners would hear cases related to escaped slaves. The commissioners would be paid twice as much money for their work if a slave was returned to the slaveholder than if the slave was freed. Passage of the Fugitive Slave Act greatly increased the number of hunts for fugitive slaves.

In 1854, Congress passed the Kansas-Nebraska Act, which allowed white males who lived in those territories to vote on whether or not they would permit slavery. When Andrew Horatio Reeder, the first territorial governor of Kansas, arrived in 1854, he found that there were more "Free Soil" (antislavery) settlers in Kansas than there were proslavery settlers. Yet when elections were held to form a state legislature, the proslavery people won decisively. It soon became clear that the elections were a fraud. Hundreds of proslavery men from neighboring Missouri had come to Kansas to vote illegally. Outraged Free-Soilers set up their own Kansas government in October 1855.

When a proslavery settler murdered a Free-Soiler, violence erupted along the Kansas-Missouri border. Throughout the territory, Free-Soilers and proslavery forces faced off. This small-scale civil war, which came to be known as "Bleeding Kansas," only made divisions worse across the United States.

In 1857, the U.S. Supreme Court handed down its decision on the court case *Dred Scott v. Sandford.* Dred Scott was a slave whose owner had taken him to live for some years in free territories. On that basis, Scott believed he could successfully sue for his freedom. However, the Supreme Court decided that because Scott was African American, he could not be a U.S. citizen or exercise a citizen's right to sue. He would remain a slave. This decision was a great blow to the antislavery cause.

DEBATES AND DEFIANCE

By 1858, slavery had become an urgent subject on the political scene. In Illinois, Stephen Douglas was up for reelection in the Senate. Running against him was a lawyer named Abraham Lincoln who challenged Douglas to a series of seven debates on the subject of slavery.

Lincoln declared that the Union would collapse if all the states did not live under the same laws regarding slavery. He went on to say that "there is no reason why the Negro is not entitled to all the natural rights enumerated in the Declaration of Independence. . . ." After the debates, Douglas won reelection to his Senate seat. He would try for the presidency in 1860.

In 1859, an abolitionist named John Brown led a group of about 50 men and boys to Harpers Ferry, Virginia, where they seized a federal arsenal. They intended to use the armaments stored there to attack Virginia slaveholders. Brown and his group were quickly arrested by federal and state troops. On December 2, 1859, Brown was hanged for his actions. Because of his abolitionist views, many considered him a martyr for the cause of freedom. Thousands of Northerners who had earlier thought little about slavery became abolitionists.

In the election of 1860, Lincoln was the Republican Party's candidate for president. The party's campaign took an antislavery stand that focused on keeping slavery out of the territories. John Brown's influence probably added many votes for Lincoln in the balloting. Lincoln won the election, so it was he and not Stephen Douglas who would face the challenge of the war.

The Civil War began on April 12, 1861, in Charleston, South Carolina, when General P. G. T. Beauregard ordered his soldiers to fire on Fort Sumter. The fort belonged to the U.S. government. General Beauregard intended to claim the fort for the Southern states that had seceded, now called the Confederate States of America (also called the Confederacy).

Before the war ended, more than 620,000 soldiers would die. Among the dead would be some 38,000 African Americans, both slaves and free, from both the North and the South. For the African Americans, the war was not about secession or states' rights. It was about ending slavery at last.

1

The First African Americans to Serve

This 1863 engraving was used on a poster in Philadelphia, Pennsylvania, to recruit African Americans for the Union army. Blacks were not officially allowed to join the Union cause until August 1862.

THE START OF THE CIVIL WAR

When the Confederates fired on Fort Sumter, President Lincoln knew he must mobilize Union troops. As of April 12, 1861, the U.S. Army had only 17,000 soldiers. Many of these were stationed in the Western territories. President Lincoln called for state governors to recruit an additional 75,000 militiamen. The action at Fort Sumter produced such a wave of patriotism in the North that the response was overwhelming. Ohio's governor described the Northerners' "hurry and enthusiasm" to serve: "The lion in us is thoroughly roused," he wrote to the president.

In this picture, U.S. president Abraham Lincoln, shown in his famous top hat, visits Union general George McClellan (center foreground) and McClellan's staff in Antietam, Maryland, in 1862.

The governors recruited only white men, but African Americans in the Northern states were no less enthusiastic. They firmly believed that if the North won the conflict, it would mean the end of slavery. They also thought that a victory would open the way for all black Americans to achieve equal standing with white Americans.

In the week after the attack on Fort Sumter, an African-American newspaper called *The Anglo-African* spelled out the common view held by its readers. "It must be that the key to the solution of the present difficulties," an editor wrote about the war, "is the abolition of slavery." This would not be "an act of retaliation on the master," he continued, "but as a measure of justice to the slave—the sure and permanent basis of 'a more perfect Union.'"

He and other African Americans understood that slavery did not fit with America's Declaration of Independence. That document stated "that all men are created equal, that they are endowed by their Creator with certain unalienable rights, that among these are Life, Liberty, and the pursuit of Happiness." African Americans had been enslaved and denied rights of citizenship in both the South and North because of their color. They now looked to the principles on which the United States was built for fair treatment.

Officially, the Civil War had nothing to do with slavery. North and South fought over the right of states to secede from the Union. Yet most people knew that slavery played a large part in tearing the United States in two. Separate governments and separate military forces now stood ready to fight each another because slaveholders wanted to carry slavery into new territories.

As Northern whites flocked to enlist in the Union army, Northern blacks hurried to offer their services as well. By fighting alongside the white soldiers, they expected to win freedom and equality for all African Americans and prove they were just as brave, strong, and loyal as any white person. In other words, they were just as worthy as whites of the equality they sought.

AFRICAN-AMERICAN SOLDIERS REJECTED

Offers poured into state and federal offices from African Americans wanting to enlist or raise black troops for the war effort. Letters arrived from many cities: Washington, D.C.; Philadelphia and Pittsburgh, Pennsylvania; Cleveland and Cincinnati, Ohio; New York City; and Boston, Massachusetts. In many of these cities, African Americans gathered to form military organizations and drill companies. They wanted to be ready to fight.

One black man from Boston, making a case for black enlistments in a letter to the War Department, wrote that "there is not a man who would not leap for his knapsack and musket." Black soldiers, he explained, "would make it hot for old Virginia." In another letter, two black men from Massachusetts declared that they had supported Lincoln's election: "The question now is will you allow us the poor privilege of fighting—and (if need be) dying—to support those in office who are our own choice." Other African Americans hoped to make the idea of black troops more acceptable to white leaders by suggesting that black soldiers be put under the leadership of white officers.

Despite the African Americans' best efforts, Lincoln and his government refused to see the war as an opportunity for African Americans to gain equality. As one editor for a Massachusetts newspaper, *The Republican,* said, "if there is one point of honor upon which more than another this [Lincoln] administration will stick, it is its pledge not to interfere with slavery in the states." Lincoln had not even suggested that free blacks should be equal. One group of African Americans after another met with rejection. Some of those seeking to enlist were even greeted with violence.

For the Union's Cause

Even before the Union began to enlist African Americans, black men joined the Civil War effort. They became servants and laborers for the military. If their skin color was light enough, they often claimed to be white and enlisted.

Nicholas Biddle, a free African American from Pennsylvania, joined a brigade called the Washington Artillerists. The week after the attack on Fort Sumter, this brigade marched through Baltimore, Maryland, on its way to defend Washington, D.C. Because the people in Baltimore sided strongly with the South, they were furious to see Union troops marching through their city, especially with a black man in their group. They began to mock the soldiers. Then they threw stones and bricks at the men, aiming especially for Biddle. One rock hit him full in the face, leaving him unsteady and bleeding. When the artillerists arrived that night in the capital, Abraham Lincoln is said to have visited them to offer his thanks. He saved a special word of sympathy for Biddle, who was one of the first Union men to bleed for the cause.

Lincoln had made plain over many years that he did not approve of slavery. Yet as the nation's leader, he had promised to leave slavery alone where it already existed. It remained one of the many issues that state governments decided for themselves, rather than having the national government decide for them. As the nation went to war with itself, some slaveholding states in the Upper South, called border states, remained loyal to the Union. Lincoln feared that he would anger the citizens of these states if he armed African Americans, so he refused all offers of black enlistment. African Americans received letters stating, "This [War] Department has no intention at present to call into the service of the Government any colored soldiers."

Some African Americans with light-colored skin responded to the government's decision by hiding their African lineage. When they went to enlist in the Union army, they pretended to be white men and gave false information about their hometowns, occupations, and families. The Union officers were happy to welcome these recruits.

WORKING FOR THE CONFEDERACY

In the South, meanwhile, the start of the war gave many slaves the courage to run for freedom. They believed that once they were behind Union lines, they would be protected. Yet in the early weeks of the war, Northern generals often returned these slaves to their masters. Brigadier General Benjamin F. Butler even offered his troops in the border state of Maryland to help stop a suspected slave uprising. General George B. McClellan, preparing to march against Confederates in western Virginia, gave orders to his officers that made clear they were not to help the slaves. "See that the rights and property of the people are respected," he instructed, referring to the slaves as "property." He went on to say that the Union army must "repress," or stop, "all attempts at Negro insurrection."

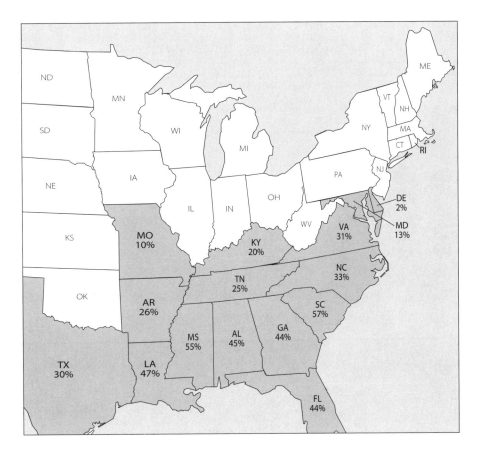

Overall, one out of every three people in the South was a slave. This map shows the percentage of each state's population that were slaves. Only in Mississippi and South Carolina did slaves outnumber white people. For this reason, African Americans could not hope to win their freedom through violent rebellion.

Such incidents gave many Southern blacks doubts about the Union's cause. As a result, some African Americans in the South, both free and enslaved, decided to offer their services to the Confederate army. The slaves were "determined to fight for the South, in the hope that their masters may set them free after the war," as one letter from a former Southern slave to an abolitionist explained. Most did not believe that they could successfully rebel against the slaveholders, so they put their hope in being freed for their loyalty.

As shown in this illustration, during the Civil War, slaves often worked for the Confederate army with the idea that they would be freed after the war for demonstrating such loyalty.

The free blacks of New Orleans went so far as to form a military organization called the Native Guards. These armed men became part of Louisiana's state militia, though the Confederate army never called on them to fight. The Native Guards had seen free Southern blacks who supported the North driven out of their homes and businesses. They did not want to share that fate. In addition, some of the New Orleans freemen actually owned slaves themselves. They had an interest in maintaining the slave culture.

Southern leaders were willing to give free blacks work in the Confederate army, but not as soldiers. Whether free or enslaved, the African Americans who served the Confederacy became army laborers, building fortifications and erecting protective earthworks, caring for the horses, cooking for the white soldiers, and otherwise doing the work of servants.

THE ABOLITIONISTS' CAUSE

Long before the Civil War began, abolitionists had spoken out against slavery and worked to make it illegal. The coming of the war gave new hope and energy to their efforts. Black and white, North and South, they poured out newspaper articles, pamphlets, lectures, songs, and sermons. Their message was simple: In the words of the Declaration of Independence, blacks' "title to life, to liberty and the pursuit of happiness must be acknowledged, or the nation" would be lost. The time for emancipation, or freedom from enslavement, had arrived.

An escaped slave himself, abolitionist Frederick Douglass always spoke out strongly against the evils of slavery.

One of the most important abolitionists, Frederick Douglass, had once been a slave himself. As far as Douglass and his fellow abolitionists were concerned, emancipation of all slaves was the only right outcome of the war. Not only that, it was the only way to win the war. He declared,

To our mind, there is but one easy, short and effectual way to suppress and put down the desolating war which the slave-holders and their rebel minions are now waging against the American Government and its loyal citizens. Fire must be met with water, darkness with light and war for the destruction of liberty must be met with war for the destruction of slavery. The simple way, then, to put on an end to the savage and desolating war now waged by the slaveholders, is to strike down slavery itself, *the primal cause of that war.*

Douglass understood that slavery gave the Confederacy strength. Slaves worked the fields to keep cash crops growing and food available. Their labor freed able-bodied white men to fill the Confederate military ranks. "Why, in the name of all that is national," Douglass demanded, "does our Government allow its enemies this powerful advantage?"

Douglass and other abolitionists made this practical argument in favor of arming blacks and ending slavery in order to convince Lincoln to change the government's policies. They wanted the army to stop sending fugitive slaves back to their masters. They wanted African Americans to be able to fight against the states that were determined to keep slavery alive. They also wanted, of course, slavery to be made illegal everywhere in the United States.

Black abolitionists' goals went beyond winning the war, though, and even beyond emancipation. They wanted equal standing with whites. "Once let the black man get upon his person the brass letters, U.S.," said Douglass. "Let him get an eagle on his button, and a musket on his shoulder and bullets in his pockets, and there is no power on earth which can deny that he has earned the right to citizenship in the United States." In other words, if the Union would allow African Americans to fight for it, the blacks would show that they deserved equal rights in all ways.

At age 20, Frederick Douglass impersonated a sailor and escaped from the Baltimore slaveholders who owned him. By the time of the Civil War, 23 years later, he had founded and published his own newspaper, *The North Star*, written three autobiographies, and become a well-known spokesman for antislavery and women's rights. He also served, at times, as a trusted adviser to President Lincoln.

IN FAVOR OF BLACK SOLDIERS

African Americans and abolitionists were not the only ones who saw advantages in allowing blacks to become U.S. soldiers. Officers in the armed services wanted to advance up the ranks. For them, regiments of African Americans offered new possibilities for advancement. Not all white officers had the inclination or willingness to lead black troops, so an officer of lower rank might have a better chance of being promoted if he was willing to take the job.

"Black Dispatches"

In 1863, Confederate general Robert E. Lee wrote, "The chief source of information to the enemy is through our Negroes." He was absolutely correct. Because most African Americans were slaves or servants, the white people they served took their presence for granted and often spoke freely in front of them. The slaves recognized any valuable information and were prepared to carry that information to the Union army. The blacks knew the locations of Confederate troops. They also knew about roads, railroads, supplies, and troop movements. Union men called the information the slaves offered "black dispatches." (A dispatch is an important official message.)

Frederick Douglass would write,

The true history of the war will show that the loyal army found no friends at the South so faithful, active, and daring in their efforts to sustain the government as the Negroes. . . . Negroes have repeatedly threaded their way through the lines of the rebels exposing themselves to bullets to convey important information to the loyal army of the Potomac.

Some people argued, as well, that blacks in the Union army would have a strong negative effect on Southern troops. Many Southerners believed that African Americans would gladly kill whites in retaliation for the sufferings of slavery. Facing armed African Americans in battle, supporters of black troops proclaimed, would terrify the Southern troops. This would give the Northern army an advantage. Many people also believed that African Americans were better able than Northern whites to handle the climate of the Deep South, which was similar to that of Africa, and to resist such diseases as malaria. If Northern troops must march into such conditions, they thought, black troops would be more likely to survive.

Other people realized that every black American who was allowed to enlist could take the place of a white American. If blacks were allowed to go into battle, fewer white soldiers would have to die. Such an argument showed that racism existed in the North just as certainly as it did in the South. The African Americans were willing to put up with such ugly ideas if it meant that they could prove themselves in battle.

THE FIRST CONFISCATION ACT

On May 23, 1861, three slaves escaped to the Union army's Fort Monroe in Virginia. The following day, the slaves' owner demanded that the commanding officer, General Benjamin Butler, return the slaves to him according to the Fugitive Slave Act. General Butler refused. Virginia had seceded from the Union, he said, and therefore had no legal rights under U.S. law. The slaves were contraband, or prizes of war. In other words, they now "belonged" to the United States. The term *contraband* would be used for the rest of the war to refer to slaves who escaped to Union forces.

On August 6, 1861, members of Congress made Butler's statement law by signing the First Confiscation Act. Congress described the new law as "an act to confiscate property used for insurrectionary purposes." It stated that any property (including slaves) used to help the South fight against the U.S. government could be seized by the United States. This meant that any slaves put to work for the Confederate war effort could be taken from their owners permanently. The act did not proclaim that the slaves were freed, but it allowed them to stay behind Union lines.

Meanwhile, abolitionists continued to clamor for emancipation. A well-known abolitionist named Wendell Phillips spent the winter of 1861–1862 traveling throughout the North, giving lectures to packed crowds of listeners on the evils of slavery and the need to end it. In March 1862, he spoke to audiences in Washington, D.C. Among his listeners were the president and members of Congress.

Perhaps Phillips convinced some of his listeners in the government of his argument, because later that month Congress passed a new article of war that made it illegal for army officers to return fugitive slaves to their masters. It also passed a resolution offering to pay compensation to "any state which may adopt gradual abolishment of slavery." It directed this offer especially to the border states that continued to support the Union.

2

African Americans' Right to Fight

This 1863 cartoon shows a black man appealing to
President Abraham Lincoln to fight for the Union while troops march
into a raging battle behind them.

Robert Smalls was an enslaved African American in South Carolina when the Civil War broke out. Hired out by his master to work in Charleston's shipyard, he became a pilot on a steam-powered paddleboat called the *Planter,* which sailed South Carolina's coastal waters.

By 1862, the Union navy had set up a blockade along the South Carolina coast to stop all Confederate shipping. The *Planter,* meanwhile, had been chartered by the Confederate government to carry important military supplies through the shallow waters just off the coast.

Early on May 13, Smalls, his wife, his three children, and eight other slaves stole the *Planter.* Smalls guided the vessel within range of the Union navy's fleet and offered the boat to the Union officers. He delivered not only the vessel, cargo, armaments, and cannon but also vital information about the Confederate defenses. Smalls went on to serve the Union in 17 engagements, and he eventually became a captain in the Union navy. He later learned to read, served in the South Carolina legislature, and was elected to five terms as a U.S. Representative.

AFRICAN AMERICANS AND THE U.S. ARMY

In the Union army, the increasing number of contrabands caused mixed feelings. Officers found the African Americans' local knowledge helpful. The slaves offered their services as spies and guides through areas that Northern officers knew nothing about. White soldiers also liked having African Americans available to do noncombat work, which they hated doing. As one Maine soldier encamped in Louisiana explained in a letter home, "Officers and men are having an easy time. We have Negroes to do all fatigue work, cooking and washing clothes." (Fatigue duty was all the noncombat, manual work that had to be done in the military.)

Many officers, however, grumbled that the growing numbers of fugitives in camp slowed down the movement of their troops and used up supplies that should have gone to the white soldiers. Although a lot of the young soldiers objected to slavery, they did not all care about African Americans as people. Some men treated the fugitives kindly and were glad that the former slaves would no longer be sent back to their masters to be punished. Other soldiers were disrespectful or even cruel. Stories circulated of white soldiers badly mistreating and hurting black men, women, and children.

Despite the reactions of officers and soldiers, tens of thousands of black men and women poured into Union camps. By the summer of 1862, large numbers of African Americans had been put to work for both the navy and army. They helped to build fortifications and prepare camps. They drove wagons, chopped wood, and cleared roads. They also cooked meals, did laundry, and nursed injured and sick men in makeshift hospitals. Even without being allowed to fight, they performed vital services to keep the Union forces going.

THE BEGINNING OF CHANGE

Even though Secretary of the Navy Welles had authorized navy officers to enlist blacks as sailors in the fall of 1861, Congress continued to debate the question of arming African Americans. Other Northerners looked ahead to when the war would end. As the Union forces took control of the Southern coast, slaveholders fled their plantations, leaving property and slaves behind. This raised the question of what would become of the thousands of abandoned African Americans who owned little or nothing and rarely knew how to read or write.

Soon, volunteer teachers and missionaries began to arrive from such organizations as the New England Freedman's Aid Society. The volunteers hoped to help the former slaves adjust to life as free people. Successful volunteer work on South Carolina's Sea Islands came to be viewed as a grand experiment in the crusade for emancipation. There, former slaves learned to read and write, ran farms for themselves, and developed skills that would allow them to live independently and earn a living. "Although the war has not been waged against slavery," said Secretary of State William Seward, "yet the army acts . . . as an emancipating crusade."

Meanwhile, some Union officers were ready and eager to arm African-American soldiers. They did not want to wait for the president's official permission, which seemed slow in coming. In May 1862, General David Hunter, the officer in charge of the Union army occupation in South Carolina, Georgia, and Florida, set out to raise a regiment of freedmen. He issued his own emancipation proclamation, and shortly afterward organized the First South Carolina Colored Regiment. Although many Northern and Southern blacks longed to fight, Hunter's efforts did not produce the troops he expected. Some black men came forward willingly, but many others held back, fearing for the families they would leave behind in slave country. Hunter could not gather enough men to fill the ranks.

Hunter then instituted a draft and brought many African Americans into his new regiment by force. This frightened and angered many of the black recruits and sent other freedmen into hiding. When Congress heard what Hunter had done without government approval, it refused to give his black regiment supplies or pay. All but one of Hunter's African-American companies had to be disbanded.

In Kansas, General James H. Lane raised two regiments of black soldiers. Some of these men had fled from Missouri to escape slavery. Others were already free and had traveled from the North to participate. The War Department refused to recognize the troops, but the African Americans fought anyway, battling the proslavery troublemakers who roamed the countryside of Kansas and Missouri.

After Union forces took control of New Orleans in the spring of 1862, General Butler received an offer of service from the Native Guards, the Confederate regiment of free African Americans that had been formed before the Union army's arrival. Although Butler would not accept the offer at first, he came back to the Guards for help when Confederate troops threatened to attack. To the U.S. government, he argued that he had not recruited these soldiers. They were already soldiers; the men had just changed the side they were fighting for. Again, the War

Black officers and soldiers served the Louisiana regiments, but the officers were forced to resign once they joined the Union army. Union troops were too prejudiced to accept black leaders. Only after the Civil War did the U.S. government let black officers lead troops into combat.

Department did not recognize the black troops, and again they fought anyway.

When a group of African Americans from Indiana offered the Union two regiments in 1862, President Lincoln made his viewpoint clear once again. "To arm the Negroes," he declared, "would turn 50,000 bayonets from the border states against us that were for us." He also expressed his doubts that black soldiers could stand against Confederate troops in battle. "If we were to arm [the African Americans]," he said, "I fear that in a few weeks the arms would be in the hands of the rebels."

THE U.S. GOVERNMENT TAKES ACTION

In the North, public opinion was beginning to shift. Northerners had thought that the war would be over in weeks or months at most. By the summer of 1862, however, the fighting had continued for more than a year, and there was no end in sight. As the Union suffered one military defeat after another, white men became much less eager to enlist. More and more people began to ask why African Americans should not join in the fight.

Finally, on July 17, 1862, Congress took action, passing the Second Confiscation Act, which allowed the United States to confiscate any Confederate property, even if it had not been used in the war. This meant that all slaves in the South could now be taken from their masters. The act also allowed the president "to employ as many persons of African descent as he may deem necessary and proper for the suppression of this rebellion."

After August 1862, blacks could officially serve in the Union army. This wood engraving that appeared in *Harper's Weekly* magazine in March 1863 shows a white officer training black recruits to use a Minie rifle.

On the same day, Congress approved the Militia Act, which repealed a law from 1792 stating that black men could not serve. Under the new law, free and freed African Americans could be employed as soldiers. At last, the door was open to officially enlisting African Americans.

On August 25, 1862, the War Department officially authorized the mustering of African Americans as soldiers, even though some black men had already fought for the North and served as laborers in the South. The orders from Secretary of War Edwin M. Stanton went to General Rufus Saxton in the Sea Islands of South Carolina. Saxton was ordered "to arm, uniform, equip, and receive into the service of the United States such number of volunteers of African descent as you may deem expedient, not exceeding 5,000, and . . . detail officers to instruct them in military drill, discipline, and duty, and to command them." Stanton went on to say that "persons so received into service and their officers [are] to be entitled to and [will] receive the same pay and rations as are allowed by law to volunteers in the service." The federal government did not honor this promise of equal pay and rations at first. In fact, for two years, it was treated as a mistake made by the secretary of war. Even so, African Americans had finally received the right to fight.

African Americans on the Run

George E. Stephens, a Northern black man serving as a Union cook, wrote in November 1862 about the hardships suffered by the fugitive slaves who followed the Federal troops, seeking freedom:

George and Kitty Washington and four remaining children belonged, with seventy others, to a man named Joe Weaver. . . . Our forces evacuated that place yesterday morning. Weaver had carried off to Richmond [Virginia] two other children of Washington, but our troops came on him before he could get the rest away. Kitty knew as soon as the Union soldiers left that she and her children would be carried down South, so she took as many of her things as she and her husband could conveniently carry and turned her steps northward. Her little children walked so slow that the rebel cavalry watching the movement of our troops came near to capturing them; but they struck the woods, and reached here in the drenching rain about 12 o'clock. . . . They also stated that all Negroes caught attempting to escape are ordered to be shot.

President Lincoln wanted his announcement of the Emancipation Proclamation to follow a big Union military victory. He got the victory when the Union defeated the Confederate army at the Battle of Antietam in Maryland on September 17, 1862.

A month earlier, President Lincoln had begun to talk with other Union leaders about taking a stronger stand against slavery. He proposed an Emancipation Proclamation that would free slaves in any state that remained part of the Confederacy as of January 1, 1863. This would not include slaves in the border states that continued to be loyal to the Union. Neither would it include slaves in states or regions already occupied by Union forces. As far as the Union was concerned, however, all slaves in states still in the possession of the Confederates by the first of the year would be free.

Lincoln knew that the reaction to the proclamation would be dramatic. For the first time, slavery would become an

Mathew Brady was the most famous of a number of photographers who carried images of the Civil War to the Northern public. Photographs showed civilians the true horrors of the battlefield. Brady's photos increased the North's feelings against the Confederacy.

official cause of the war. Some people would cheer in favor of the decision, and others would protest against it. Lincoln believed that his proclamation would be most convincing to Southern leaders if it followed a decisive military victory for the Union, so he waited before announcing it.

Lincoln got what he wanted on September 17, 1862, when Union general George McClellan defeated Robert E. Lee at Antietam in Maryland. Lee had intended to invade the North. At Antietam, McClellan stopped him at great cost to both armies. The Union forces lost 2,108 men, with 9,549 wounded and 753 missing. The South had 2,700 killed, 9,024 wounded, and 2,000 missing.

On September 22, Lincoln issued the first draft of the Emancipation Proclamation. News traveled quickly that it would be signed into law on January 1, 1863. In the South, slaveholders worried that slaves would stage a large rebellion sometime between Christmas and January 1. Slaves and free people of color, meanwhile, prepared for New Year's celebrations. Officers of a black military organization in New Orleans planned to hold a "Large procession" on New Year's Day and a "Grand union Dinner" on January 2, the profits of which they would give to "the poor people in the Camp [the contraband camp outside New Orleans], the colored Women and children."

3

Raising the "U.S. Colored Troops"

In this 1867 steel engraving, the 54th Massachusetts Volunteer Infantry Regiment, which was black, leads the charge on Fort Wagner in South Carolina on July 18, 1863. The men inspired others with their bravery though the battle was lost.

EMANCIPATION BECOMES LAW

On January 1, 1863, President Lincoln signed the Emancipation Proclamation into law. The proclamation freed only those slaves who lived in the Confederate states that remained "in rebellion against the United States." It further declared that "the Executive government of the United States, including the military and naval authorities thereof, will recognize and maintain the freedom of said persons." In other words, no slaves would ever again be sent back to their former masters.

People in both the North and South continued to fear that former slaves, once freed, would take up weapons and turn against the masters who had kept them in slavery. People worried, as well, that the African Americans would look to the government to support them. To discourage such events, Lincoln had added to the earlier version of the proclamation that the freed slaves should avoid "all violence, unless in necessary self-defense," and should "labor faithfully for reasonable wages."

Lincoln made another important addition to the proclamation. He stated that "such [black freed] persons of suitable condition, will be received into the armed service of the United States to garrison forts, positions, stations, and other places, and to man vessels of all sorts in said service." By law, states could now call on their black citizens and fugitive slaves to serve in the military as armed soldiers and sailors.

By the end of the war, the U.S. military would raise six regiments of U.S. Colored Cavalry, eleven regiments and four companies of U.S. Colored Heavy Artillery, ten batteries of

U.S. Colored Light Artillery, and 100 regiments and 16 companies of U.S. Colored Infantry (foot soldiers). In all, historians believe that as many as 190,000 black soldiers and sailors served in the Union forces.

Thousands of blacks served in the Union forces by the end of the war. They performed every kind of duty from cooking meals to fighting on the front lines.

EMANCIPATION DAY

Word of the coming Emancipation Proclamation had spread far and wide in the days between September 22 and January 1. Throughout the North and parts of the South, African

Americans gathered on New Year's Eve in what they would later call watch night services. They waited together for the moment that slavery would finally be brought to an end in the Confederate states, a moment that America's slaves had awaited for almost 250 years.

Through the night, people prayed, sang, danced, and paraded, joining together in choruses of "Forever free! Forever free!" and "My country 'tis of thee." In the morning, the announcement was spread by telegraph and newspapers that the president had issued his proclamation. Word quickly circulated that this new version of the proclamation officially allowed African Americans to bear arms for their country. At last, they could prove their loyalty and courage in action.

African Americans understood that the proclamation was only the beginning. In Harrisburg, Pennsylvania, a group of black citizens gathered two weeks later to consider what the proclamation would mean to them. They opened their meeting by singing a song called "Year of Jubilee Has Come." The term *jubilee* came from a law in the Bible that declared that every 50 years, all Hebrew people in slavery must be set free.

After discussing the Emancipation Proclamation, the Harrisburg group wrote a list of their responses. They said that "we, the colored citizens of the city of Harrisburg, hail the 1st day of January, 1863, as a new era in our country's history—a day in which injustice and oppression were forced to flee . . . before the . . . principles of justice and righteousness." They stated that they would have chosen that all slaves be freed right away. Yet they could see freedom for all in the future and could still say that "the American flag is now a true emblem of liberty."

Throughout the Americas, emancipated slaves created holidays to celebrate the time when they were freed. In the British Caribbean islands, August 1 became the traditional day of jubilee. On that day in 1834, a law passed the previous year went into effect, and slavery everywhere in British lands was abolished. France followed England's example and ended slavery in all its American territories in 1848. The Spanish did not emancipate their slaves until 1880, and Brazil ended slavery only in 1888. Some former slave societies chose different days to remember emancipation, but they all developed celebrations.

In the United States, January 1 continues to be celebrated as the commemorative day of freedom. However, millions of U.S. slaves did not enjoy the emancipation proclaimed by Lincoln on that day. Emancipation would not be complete until the Civil War ended. That is why many African Americans also observe the day known as "Juneteenth" (June 19, 1865), which is considered the date when the last slaves in the United States heard the news that they were free. All the celebrations on this day honor freedom and aim to make sure that slavery is never forgotten or again tolerated.

The reactions of the African Americans in Harrisburg were repeated in black churches and meeting places wherever the proclamation was read. African Americans throughout the states came to call the day of emancipation their "Day of Jubilee." They believed, as the Harrisburg group had written, that "freedom and citizenship are attended with responsibilities . . . the success or failure of the proclamation depends entirely upon ourselves." They must act like free citizens if they wanted to be treated like free citizens. Such actions included the willingness to fight for their country.

As news of the Emancipation Proclamation spread south, fugitive slave families took courage from it and fled behind Union lines in larger and larger numbers. Some had help from sympathetic African Americans and whites along the way. Such people were willing to hide slaves when they stopped to rest, provide them with food and supplies, and sometimes guide the runaways to the next safe place on the way north. This informal organization of helpers came to be known as the Underground Railroad. Many fugitives hoped to reach Canada and other northern destinations. Others remained close to Union troops, hoping to join the Union cause.

AFRICAN AMERICANS TO ARMS!

After two years of war, the white population of the Union was ready for black soldiers in its army and navy. As army chaplain George H. Hepworth wrote, "We needed that the vast tide of death should roll by our own doors and sweep away our fathers and sons, before we could come to our senses and give the black man . . . permission to fight for our common country."

For the African Americans, the right to fight had more importance than simply winning the war. Serving in the Union forces would be an example and an inspiration to future generations. One black volunteer in South Carolina expressed it this way: "Suppose you had kept your freedom without enlisting in this army. Your children might have grown up free and been well cultivated to be equal to any business; but it would have been always flung in their faces— 'Your father never fought for his own freedom.'"

Before the end of January 1863, Secretary of War Stanton had authorized state governors to enlist black troops. The governor of Massachusetts, John A. Andrew, chose a number of well-known black leaders to act as recruiting agents. The most famous of these leaders was Frederick Douglass. Douglass took on the task with enthusiasm. He and other leaders recruited blacks by giving public lectures, going from house to house, and visiting general stores, barber shops, and churches—wherever able-bodied black men could be found.

Within weeks, African Americans were arriving at naval shipyards and army barracks, ready to sign up. Massachusetts raised the first

The Recruit is a wood engraving of a black Civil War recruit modeled after a painting by Thomas Waterman Wood.

black regiment. Rhode Island recruited the first African-American artillery regiment. Pennsylvania was slower to allow blacks into the military. The state's white leaders became more willing after Confederate troops under General Lee invaded southeastern Pennsylvania to fight the Battle of Gettysburg in the summer of 1863. African Americans, for their part, ignored the prejudice against them and expressed

Many white laborers feared that if they were drafted into the army, African Americans would take their jobs. Riots erupted in a number of Northern cities. Dozens of houses were destroyed, black people were murdered, and the Colored Orphan Asylum in New York City was burned down.

"our willingness and readiness to come forward to the defense of our imperiled country." Recruitment of black soldiers in the North spread from state to state, increasing Union forces by the thousands.

Meanwhile, Union leaders stationed in the South did their share of recruiting as well. When Edward A. Wild was named brigadier general of volunteers on April 24, 1863, he set out to draw enlistees from the Confederate states of North Carolina and Virginia. Wild was a fervent abolitionist who took seriously the need to let African Americans fight. He took charge of all black recruits in the area, called them "Wild's African Brigade," and commanded them until the war ended. In addition to serving the Union in combat, the black recruits also acted as anti-guerrilla troops, striking at the homes and property of Confederates who were secretly working against the Union.

Other Union recruiters followed Wild in enlisting and training as many free and freed African Americans in Confederate territory as they could. As they moved through the Southern plantations whose owners had fled before the Union advance, they enlisted newly freed black men and sent black women and children north to contraband camps.

On May 22, 1863, the U.S. War Department established the Bureau of Colored Troops. This bureau was created to oversee efforts to recruit black Americans throughout the nation. From that time forward, all black troops would be called United States Colored Troops. The bureau's first job was to choose more officers, all of them white, to recruit and lead future black troops. The black recruits would be organized into units which were numbered according to the order in which they were formed. By the end of 1863, enough African Americans had been recruited from the Deep South to form 30 new regiments.

Another view of the famous storming of Fort Wagner by the African-American troops of the 54th Massachusetts Regiment is shown here. The attack took place in South Carolina in July 1863.

African-American women played an active part in the Civil War. The "Women's Nurses for the Union" employed some 4,000 black women at $10 a month for their hospital work. Susie King Taylor was one of the many African Americans who worked alongside Clara Barton, the founder of the Red Cross, tending sick and wounded soldiers at the scene of battle. The navy hospital ship *Red Rover* listed at least nine African-American women serving as nurses and laundresses.

Black women also brought intelligence about the South to Union officers. Many historians believe that Elizabeth Bowser spied for the Union while she was working as a servant for Jefferson Davis, the president of the Confederacy, in Richmond. Abolitionists Sojourner Truth and Harriet Tubman both worked as scouts and nurses.

Because prejudice against African Americans did not end with the Civil War, the bravery and hard work of black women received little attention for many years. Only recently have people begun to retell the tales of African-American women who helped the Union efforts.

Some white military men questioned whether black enlistees would have the ability or the courage to fight. These whites knew that the Union army needed the manpower that the African Americans would provide. At the same time, the whites feared that people who had lived as second-class citizens, or worse, as slaves, would not be up to the task of fighting for the Union. The African Americans' long history as servants who were not allowed to bear arms would not have prepared them to fight as needed on a battlefield.

In Kansas, military leaders had recruited black soldiers despite the government's delay. These black troops had already proven their ability through the first half of 1863. On July 17, 1863, the First Kansas Colored Regiment fought under General James Blunt in the Battle of Honey Springs in what is now Oklahoma. They met enemy fire head-on and held the Union line until the Confederate troops broke rank and ran for cover.

After the battle, General Blunt had substantial praise for his African-American troops. "I never saw such fighting as was done by the Negro regiment," he exclaimed. "The question that Negroes will fight is settled . . . they make better soldiers in every respect than any troops I have ever had under my command."

The 54th Massachusetts, another African-American regiment, fought the following day in what would become a famous battle at Fort Wagner in South Carolina. The 54th's leader, Colonel Robert Gould Shaw, pleaded with his brigade commander to let the 54th actually lead the assault on the fort. Permission was granted, and the black regiment fought with heroic strength and determination. The 54th lost the battle, however, and half the regiment, including Colonel Shaw, was killed, yet word quickly spread throughout the Union of the men's bravery. After that battle, the magazine *Atlantic Monthly* proclaimed: "Through the cannon smoke of that dark night, the manhood of the colored race shines before many eyes that would not see." In light of the 54th's performance, Lincoln addressed government leaders who opposed the use of black troops, saying: "There will be some black men who can remember that, with silent tongue, and clenched teeth, and steady eye, and well-poised bayonet, they have helped mankind."

CONTRABAND CAMPS

While able-bodied African-American freedmen joined the fighting forces, their wives, children, and elderly parents fled or were sent to the Union's contraband camps to find food, shelter, and other necessities. One of the largest contraband camps, called Freedmen's Village, was located on the banks of the Potomac River in Washington, D.C. The government allowed the residents of Freedmen's Village to create a community that could support itself. The African Americans built a school, a chapel, and a hospital. They built houses and raised their own food.

Most other contraband camps did not turn out so well. They quickly became too crowded, and disease spread. Many African Americans arrived with nothing more than the clothes on their backs, and even these were often threadbare. Others came in wagons, carrying tools, animals, and clothes with them. In the South, camps were often set up on abandoned plantations. The people crowded into small quarters and often worked nearly as hard as they had as slaves, raising food and serving the needs of the Union troops under the supervision of white officers. They never forgot the big difference, though. Now they were free.

4

Racism in the Ranks, North and South

This illustration shows black troops being addressed by white superiors in Nashville, Tennessee, in 1864. Black troops were often subjected to racism by their white peers in the Union army.

RACISM IN THE RANKS

The Emancipation Proclamation legally freed many slaves. The proclamation also made the recruitment of black soldiers and sailors official. Yet it could not stop the effects of racism. African Americans continued to be treated differently from whites, even in the military. The fact that the government called them the "U.S. Colored Troops" made clear that even the Union's leaders put them in a category of their own.

African-American soldiers are shown here on guard duty for a Union army camp during the Civil War.

As African American troops began to swell the ranks of the Union army and navy, a number of issues arose. When and how would the the black soldiers learn the skills they needed to bear arms and fight? What would they be paid? How would their families survive while they were away fighting? What sort of duties would the commanders assign to them? Just as important, what opportunities would they have to rise to positions of leadership and responsibility? Finally, what treatment could they expect at the hands of the enemy, the Confederates?

Many African Americans expected that freedom and the right to fight would give them equality with their white fellow soldiers. Nothing could have been further from the truth. In every way, they found that their battle for equality had only begun.

TRAINING FOR BATTLE

Although there were some African Americans in the front lines of battle as early as the fall of 1862, many more recruits received noncombat duty. White commanders often sent black recruits ahead of the troops as raiding parties to destroy the fortifications and supplies of the Confederates. The white commanders also assigned the black recruits to build Union fortifications along the rivers and the coast. At the same time, the blacks continued to do the fatigue duty of the encampment. This included cooking, caring for the animals, and acting as personal servants to the officers. It also meant, as one soldier described it, "digging trenches, hauling logs and cannon, [and] loading ammunition." It was often the black soldiers who had to "lay out camps, pitch tents, dig wells, etc. for white regiments who have lain idle until work was finished for them."

Such work took a lot of time and energy. It left the black soldiers little opportunity to prepare for active duty at the front. The officers who had accepted leadership of the black troops complained to their commanders. As one leader explained, these officers would rather have been foot soldiers themselves than be "overseers" to black laborers.

While recruiting African-American troops in the Mississippi valley from 1863 to the end of the war, General Lorenzo Thomas constantly encountered racism against blacks.

The government assigned General Lorenzo Thomas to recruit black troops in the Mississippi valley. Soon after his arrival, he reported that "the prejudice against colored troops was quite general, and it required in the first instance all my efforts to counteract it." Thomas's efforts received a boost from the African-American troops themselves when they protested unequal treatment. Like their officers, they wrote letters and petitions against being constantly assigned to jobs that were similar to the work they had done before they were allowed to enlist.

By 1864, General Thomas began to make needed changes on behalf of the black soldiers. He ordered that African Americans should not be overburdened with drudgery. "They will be only required to take their fair share of fatigue duty with white troops," he declared. "This is necessary to prepare them for the higher duties of conflicts with the enemies."

Eventually, the general gave credit to the African-American troops for their advancements in the military. He reported, "The blacks themselves . . . by their coolness and determination in battle fought themselves into their present high standing as soldiers." That African Americans had to prove themselves in ways that white soldiers did not was just one more form of prejudice.

AFRICAN AMERICANS IN HIGH PLACES

As a rule, African Americans were permitted to serve only in the lowest ranks of the army and navy. Frederick Douglass wrote that "it is a little cruel to say to the black soldier that he shall not rise to be an officer of the United States whatever may be his merits." Yet Douglass encouraged African Americans to enlist. "Go into the army," he said, "and go with a will and a determination to blot out this and all other mean discriminations against us."

Many black soldiers studied military tactics to prepare themselves to lead troops, but only a handful of African Americans were given rank and authority in the Union army. Out of nearly 200,000 African-American soldiers, no more than 100 (not counting chaplains) became commissioned officers (lieutenants and higher) during the war. Black officers commanded an all-black regiment recruited in Louisiana in the spring of 1863. A small number of black officers also served in other regiments. At least eight African Americans were listed among the army's hospital surgeons. Thirteen received commissions as chaplains.

The few African Americans who became commissioned officers showed great courage and loyalty. Yet their low numbers remained a bar to enlisting other black soldiers. A group of noncommissioned African-American officers from Louisiana wrote a letter on this issue to the secretary of war in Washington, D.C. They pointed out that many loyal black men hesitated to enlist "because one of the greatest incentives to enlistment, and the greatest stimulant to the strict performance of a soldier's duty—the hope of promotion—has been denied them."

ONE WOMAN'S CRUSADE

> After emancipation, Sojourner Truth said, "This is a great and glorious day! It is good to live in it and behold the shackles fall from the manacled limbs."

Many abolitionists, black and white, worked hard to break down the prejudice that surrounded African Americans in and out of the armed forces. Among them was a woman named Sojourner Truth. Once a slave herself, she waged a war of words against slavery and racism, working tirelessly in the cause of freedom. Although she could neither read nor write, she delivered powerful lectures in support of abolition and civil rights.

As more and more African Americans enlisted, Truth found out that the black troops received less food than white soldiers. In addition, they were issued weapons, supplies, and uniforms in the worst repair. Truth used the money she raised from her lectures to buy gifts, food, and clothing for the poorly supplied men. Once, she traveled in Michigan from Battle

Creek to a camp near Detroit to deliver a Thanksgiving dinner to the First Michigan Colored Infantry.

In 1863, Truth found that in Freedmen's Village, in Washington, D.C., the black soldiers' wives, parents, and children had barely enough to survive. She learned that they were forced to buy donated clothing that had been intended to be given to needy blacks for free. She also discovered that local white people were kidnapping the village's black children to enslave them. When parents complained, local authorities threw them in the military jail. Truth set out to help the parents reclaim their children by

Former slave Sojourner Truth was a passionate advocate for abolition and civil rights for African Americans.

reporting the kidnappings to the Union army and government authorities. When she, too, was threatened by Union officers with imprisonment for her activities, she threatened in return. Just try to arrest her, she declared, and she would "make this nation rock like a cradle."

In 1864, Truth's activities earned her a meeting with President Lincoln. Lincoln praised her for her work and appointed her to the National Freedmen's Relief Association.

Her activities did not cease with the end of the war. In the aftermath, she supported the idea of a black state in the West. She also supported efforts to provide jobs for the thousands and thousands of newly liberated slaves.

SIDE BY SIDE

The African-American troops showed bravery, endurance, and determination in battle after battle, winning the respect of many white soldiers. However, many other whites still continued to show how prejudiced they were. For every white soldier who sat next to a black soldier and taught him how to read and write, another 10 white soldiers refused to fight in the same regiment with an African American. In some cases, it was the African Americans who could read and write and the whites who could not—nevertheless, the white troops continued to be convinced that only whites could lead. They insisted that black soldiers should remain in segregated, or separate, regiments.

When a black surgeon was put in charge of six white surgeons who worked for the U.S. Colored Troops in Maryland, the white doctors were furious. They sent a letter to President Lincoln insisting that the black surgeon be removed. "When we made application for position in the Colored Service," they wrote, "the understanding was universal that all commissioned officers were to be white men. Judge of our surprise and disappointment when . . . we found that the Senior Surgeon of the command was a Negro." The surgeons claimed that they cared about the welfare of the African Americans. "We claim to be behind no one," they continued, "in a desire for the elevation and improvement of the Colored race. . . . But we cannot in any cause willingly compromise what we consider a proper self respect." In other words, they could only respect themselves if they disrespected the black man who had been assigned to command them.

In another case, white soldiers marching past an African-American company spotted a black officer with a lieutenant's straps on his uniform. Some of the white men shouted, "Jerk them [the straps] off, take him out, kill him." An observer stated that the white soldiers "would have dealt severely with him" if they had not been in formation.

Unequal in Life, Unequal in Death

Records from the Civil War show that the rate of African-American deaths in the conflict was 40 percent higher than that of whites. Some of these men died on the battlefield or in prisoner-of-war camps. Many more died from disease.

War historians point out that African Americans had to do extra fatigue duty, which exposed them to more injury and disease. In addition, blacks were often sent off to battle before they had been properly trained. They also received poor equipment that put them at a disadvantage when they fought. Typically, they also received worse medical care than white soldiers.

There is no question that African-American prisoners were treated much more harshly by the Confederates than if they had been white. No one knows for sure how many black deaths went unreported by Southern forces, but the total certainly added up to many thousands.

THE RIGHTS OF CITIZENSHIP

African Americans gained new hope for equality when President Lincoln signed the Emancipation Proclamation and gave them the official right to serve as full-fledged soldiers. African Americans had actually fought in every major American war, including the American Revolution (1775–1783), yet the government had never treated them as equal, free people.

Now, African Americans wanted to become full citizens of the United States, with all the rights and privileges that white people enjoyed. They wanted to be able to vote and hold public office. They wanted to have equal access to property, education, and jobs. They also wanted to receive the same fair trial promised to white citizens if they were accused of a crime. "If we fight to maintain a Republican Government," declared African-American soldier James Henry Hall, "we want Republican privileges. . . . All we ask is the proper enjoyment of the rights of citizenship." They stepped into their role as soldiers believing that they would be rewarded with those rights.

AFRICAN-AMERICAN TROOPS UNDER FIRE

The officially recognized U.S. Colored Troops fought their earliest major battles in Louisiana. On May 27, 1863, the Union army moved against the Confederates' Fort Hudson on the Mississippi River. As they attacked, African-American soldiers advanced across open ground in the face of deadly artillery fire. The attack failed, but the soldiers proved that they could fight bravely.

They proved themselves again on June 7 in one of the fiercest battles of the war. At Milliken's Bend, Confederate troops faced black regiments in close hand-to-hand combat. The African Americans had little training and were badly outnumbered and ill-equipped. Yet they won the day, making it possible for Northern troops to capture the fort at Vicksburg, Mississippi, which gave control of the Mississippi River to the Union.

On May 27, 1863, black soldiers of the Second Louisiana Regiment fought against Confederate forces at Fort Hudson in Louisiana, shown here. This was one of the first battles in which free African-American soldiers fought for the Union.

Music played an important part in the Civil War. Most regiments included a regimental band, which would play marching tunes for parades and concerts. Its music would cheer and inspire the soldiers. The music also helped in recruiting new soldiers, who would listen to the rousing songs and imagine becoming heroes in the war. Sometimes, a regiment created its own song to sing in camp or on the march. The 54th Massachusetts Regiment, which was African American, sang these words:

> So rally, boys, rally, let us never mind the past;
>
> We had a hard road to travel, but our day is coming fast;
>
> For God is for the right, and we have no need to fear,
>
> The Union must be saved by the colored volunteer.

The battle at Fort Wagner in South Carolina took place just one month later, on July 18. The 54th Massachusetts Volunteer Infantry Regiment, the first black regiment to be raised in the North, had marched hard for two days in order to take part in the attack against South Carolina's fortifications. Among the black soldiers was Sergeant Major Lewis Douglass, who was the son of Frederick Douglass. He and his regiment hoped to seize control of Charleston Harbor for the Union.

The men were tired and hungry by the time they arrived at Fort Wagner, yet they led the charge through the dark marshland in 4 feet (1.2 m) of water. The Confederates advanced against them, forcing the troops into hand-to-hand combat. Before the battle was over, 1,515 Union soldiers, including 256 of the 54th Massachusetts, had been killed or wounded. Many others were taken captive. The Union lost the battle, but the surviving men of the 54th, including Douglass, would fight again.

The black men in the Union army and navy believed that serving bravely in the military would speed them along toward equality. Yet some abolitionists, such as Sojourner Truth and Frederick Douglass, knew that fighting for the Union would not be enough to win full citizenship or respect for African Americans. Centuries of racism had denied most African Americans a basic education or a living wage. Prejudice against them continued in both the Confederacy and the Union, in the military and out of it.

Douglass knew that whites must learn to see African Americans in a new light, to see them as people just like the whites themselves. In a speech in December 1863 on suffrage, or voting rights, for black men, he challenged a meeting of the American Anti-Slavery Society, declaring that "our work will not be done until the colored man is admitted as a full member in good and regular standing in the American body politic. . . . It is said that the colored man is ignorant, and therefore he shall not vote. In saying this, you lay down a rule for the black man that you apply to no other class of your citizens."

ELECTION YEAR

As 1864 arrived, the Union faced a presidential election. Even though most African Americans did not have the right to vote, they had strong views on the election. The majority of African Americans throughout the North and South wanted Abraham Lincoln to be reelected. Many blacks made their opinions known in speeches, letters, and newspaper articles.

As early as January 1864, a huge group of African Americans gathered in San Francisco, California, and unanimously showed their support of Lincoln in a resolution. As an editorial in the newspaper *The Pacific Appeal* reported, "He is the man who, of all others who have occupied the Presidential chair . . . has stood up in defiance of the slave-power, and dared to maintain . . . that we are citizens, though of African descent."

In Baltimore, blacks showed their support for Lincoln by raising more than $580 (an enormous amount of money at the time) to purchase a special Bible to give him. On the cover was a picture of Lincoln striking the chains off a slave in a cotton field. The Reverend S. M. Chase presented the Bible to Lincoln, saying, "The loyal colored people of Baltimore . . . present this Bible as a testimonial of their appreciation of your humane conduct towards the people of our race. . . . Towards you, sir, our hearts will ever be warm with gratitude."

Black soldiers and sailors certainly wanted Lincoln to win reelection. To show their support, they bombarded African-American newspapers with letters from the battlefields that urged blacks everywhere to find ways to help Lincoln win the reelection. Their white officers did their part as well. "Do all you can for the reelection of old Abe," wrote one officer to his brother, "and you will do the best thing you can for the country's good."

FORT PILLOW

The black troops supported the president even while they faced enormous hardships and high casualties in the field. The battle at Fort Pillow in April 1864 caused less than half as many casualties as the battle at Fort Wagner, yet it stands as the most brutal battle against black troops in the Civil War. At Fort Pillow, it was reported that when the Confederate army won the battle, they refused to let any black soldiers surrender. Instead, Confederate soldiers took the blacks captive, then shot them on the spot or burned them to death.

After Union forces surrendered at Fort Pillow in April 1864, the Confederate troops mercilessly executed all the black soldiers that had fought against them.

For the remainder of the Civil War, the story of Fort Pillow would be remembered by the African-American troops, who came to believe that they would be treated the same way in other battles. Some black soldiers vowed to take revenge, promising that they would give the same brutal treatment to Confederate soldiers who surrendered. The Confederates learned to fear the attack of black troops, who would yell "Remember Fort Pillow!" as they charged.

The Confederate slaughter of African-American soldiers who had surrendered led Congress to enact strong measures to stop future horrors. The U.S. government notified Confederate officials that if they did not stop murdering or enslaving black troops, the Union would treat rebel captives in kind.

Meanwhile, black soldiers continued to fight and to support Lincoln's reelection. The presidential election was scheduled to take place in November 1864. By mid-1864, white people in the North were growing tired of the war. Thousands of men had died in the fighting, and the death toll continued to mount. Yet victory seemed no closer than at the beginning of the conflict. It was not at all certain that Lincoln would win the election unless something drastic happened to give the Union hope of a speedy victory.

THE BATTLE FOR EQUAL PAY

Even with the election approaching and the need for military victories, the U.S. government continued to discriminate against the loyal African-American troops. Unlike white soldiers, black soldiers received little or no bounty for enlisting. A bounty was a one-time sum of money given to the enlistee by the government. Soldiers often used this money to buy supplies for themselves and provide for their families in their absence.

For African-American soldiers, the rare bounty was always smaller than what was offered to a white soldier of the same rank. Often, the black soldiers never saw the money. If they joined with the permission of a former owner, that slaveholder might keep the bounty for himself. In other cases, recruiters would secretly pocket the money and lead black enlistees to believe that their freedom was the only bounty they were supposed to receive.

The Music of Hope

One of the great African-American contributions to American culture is music. Africans brought music with them from Africa, but the music changed as they lived in slavery. Because the songs used stories from the Bible about God delivering people from trouble, the songs became known as spirituals. With singing, drums, and instruments, slaves expressed the difficulty of their lives and their hope for a better future.

Northerners first heard the spirituals, which the African Americans called shout songs, in the army and contraband camps of the Civil War. Black soldiers gathered to sing their songs, as one white officer described it, "around a glimmering fire . . . in the most perfect time." Northern musicians, who found the music beautiful and strange, wrote out the melodies and lyrics and published them in magazines and booklets. As the music became known throughout the country, it conveyed the suffering of African Americans to people who had never visited a plantation or seen the terrible conditions of slavery.

As a result of lower pay than their white colleagues received, black troops, such as these shown at Bermuda Hundred, Virginia, often could not afford new uniforms or other necessities.

African-American soldiers suffered similar discrimination when it came to monthly pay for their service. White troops received $13 a month plus $3.50 as an allowance for clothes. Black troops received only seven dollars a month with a three-dollar clothing allowance, and they felt the injustice strongly. "Why are we not worth as much as white soldiers?" one man wrote to his sister. "Why is it that they do not want to give us our pay when they have already witnessed our deeds of courage and bravery?"

Both the black soldiers and their white officers objected loudly to this difference. Just like white soldiers, the black troops had families they needed to support while they were away.

The government's policy of underpaying the African-American troops led to desperate hardship for the soldiers' families, most of whom already lived in poverty. One officer of a black regiment wrote about one of his soldiers, "There is Sergeant Swails, a man who has fairly won promotion on the field of battle. . . . While he was doing the work of government in the field, his wife and children were placed in the poorhouse." Even in the freedmen camps, some people starved to death.

The white officers knew that their black soldiers fought with the same bravery and loyalty as any white troops. To deny the African Americans equal pay was not only unfair, but it put that loyalty at risk. In protest, the 54th Massachusetts Regiment went so far as to refuse any pay, rather than accept the insult of lower pay. It fought unpaid for a year.

The Third South Carolina Regiment staged a different type of protest. The men refused to fight. As a result, one of their white officers faced a court martial (a military court trial) for his part in the strike. He was charged with "leading the company to stack arms before their captain's tent." The soldiers had laid down their guns in this way to show that they considered themselves released from duty "by the refusal of the government to fulfill its share of the contract." The officer was later sentenced to be executed for his disobedience.

While the soldiers fought for equality, abolitionist civilians pressured the U.S. government to do the right thing for the African Americans. A black minister named J. P. Campbell spoke for the soldiers' rights from his Baltimore pulpit. "We ask for equal pay and bounty," he declared, "not because we set a greater value upon money than we do upon human liberty. . . . [We] contend for equal pay and bounty on principle, that if we receive equal pay and bounty when we go into the war, we hope to receive equal rights and privileges when we come out of the war."

Such declarations and protests eventually won for African Americans what they wanted. On June 15, 1864, the government finally awarded African-American troops equal pay. The news that African-American troops would receive pay equal to that of white soldiers seemed like a big step in correcting the wrongs of the past—as important as being accepted as soldiers.

6

The Proof of Their Manhood

At the Battle of Nashville, Tennessee, in December 1864, eight black regiments played a key role in helping to defeat the Confederate army.

BLACK TROOPS FIGHT

The U.S. Colored Troops fought in more than 400 engagements, 39 of which were major battles. In all, the black troops made up 10 percent of the Union forces. Some had been free and living in the North before joining the military. More were fugitive slaves from the Confederate states. One and all fought for "a double purpose," as Sergeant Major Christian A. Fleetwood wrote. African Americans enlisted, he said, "to assist in abolishing slavery and to save the country from ruin."

Not all the African Americans in the South had been enslaved. Louisiana, for example, had a large population of free blacks who had emigrated from the Caribbean. Some of these people had gained enough wealth to own plantations of their own and become slaveholders. It was from this group that the Louisiana Native Guards unit was created, and these troops joined the Union effort as soon as Louisiana fell to the North.

ON THE BATTLEGROUND

On July 22, 1864, the Union army under General William T. Sherman captured the South's second-largest city, Atlanta, Georgia. Reports of such a critical Northern victory turned the election in Lincoln's favor once and for all. The publisher of the black newspaper *The Anglo-African* wrote that "if you are a friend of liberty you will give your influence and cast your vote for Abraham Lincoln. . . ." "We are all for old Abe," wrote a black soldier from his camp in South Carolina. "Let the colored men at home do their duty."

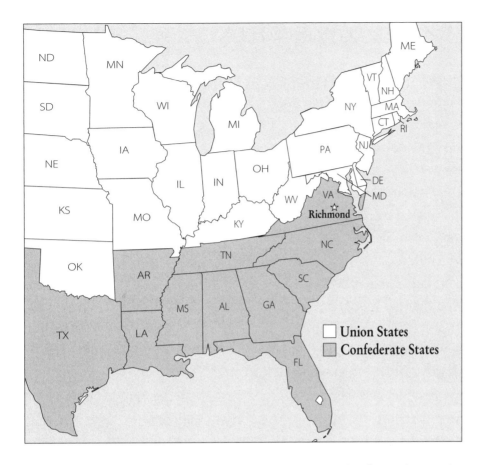

Black soldiers fought valiantly for the Union army in the Battle of Petersburg and the Battle of Chaffin's Farm. Both took place near the Confederate capital of Richmond, Virginia.

Throughout 1864, African-Americans proved themselves in battle. One battle, the Battle of the Crater, was fought on July 30, 1864, near Petersburg, Virginia. Union troops set off an explosion under a small Confederate fort, then charged into the crater that the explosion had created. They found themselves trapped under Confederate gunfire. In this battle the black troops suffered their heaviest single-day casualties of the war.

The U.S. government lists 29 members of the U.S. Colored Troops who were awarded the Congressional Medal of Honor. Most of these were African Americans.

The Medal of Honor was created during the Civil War first for the U.S. Navy on December 21, 1861. On July 14, 1862, the Army Medal of Honor was established. Congress intended that the Medal of Honor "be presented, in the name of Congress, to such non-commissioned officers and privates as shall most distinguish themselves by their gallantry in action."

African-American Medal of Honor winners were honored for many acts of soldierly bravery, including (in the words of the actual citations):

• being "among the first to enter the enemy's works [fortifications]"

• "marching through the enemy's country to bring relief"

• carrying the "colors" [flag] after the flag-bearer had been shot or the flag had fallen

• taking "command of his company, after all the officers had been killed or wounded," and gallantly leading it

• voluntarily obtaining information under heavy fire

• warning fellow troops of danger "at great personal peril"

Other battles won deepening respect for the African Americans in uniform. On September 29, two months after the Battle of the Crater, Union troops advanced on the Confederate capital of Richmond. Many would later say that the black troops were never braver than in this fight (called the Battle of Chaffin's Farm). After being caught under enemy fire and suffering many casualties, the African-American division of the 18th Corps rushed the Confederate defenses to lead the Union to victory. Fourteen black soldiers were awarded the Congressional Medal of Honor for their valor in the Battle of Chaffin's Farm, including several who took command of their units after their white commanders had fallen dead or been wounded.

GETTING READY FOR FREEDOM

Despite unfair treatment for many African Americans, joining the military offered opportunities they had never had before. Army life was always a mixture of hard marches, dangerous battles and skirmishes, and long hours of boredom. Between engagements with the enemy, soldiers had a lot of free time in the army camp. Many illiterate black soldiers put that idle time to good use by learning to read. Army chaplains, officers, and civilian teachers taught the black soldiers using Bibles or children's spelling books.

More than 9,000 black seamen served in the U.S. Navy. With their help, naval ships prevented supplies from reaching Confederate forces by sea. Naval troops also drove Confederates inland, allowing Union troops and African-American workers to use coastal plantations to produce needed food and supplies.

One such teacher was Frances Beecher, the wife of Colonel James Beecher of the 35th U.S. Colored Infantry. Frances Beecher taught many of the African-American soldiers to read and write. "It became my pleasing duty and habit," she explained, "wherever our moving tents were pitched, there to set up our school."

One officer of the 59th U.S. Colored Infantry described one such scene. "A commodious schoolhouse was built," he wrote, "where the men, when off duty, were taught . . . not only the enlisted men, but the colored women and children of the neighborhood." This instruction showed its value in the postwar lives of many African Americans. "Since the war," wrote Joseph T. Wilson of the 54th Massachusetts Regiment, "I have known of more than one who have taken up the profession of preaching and law making, whose first letter was learned in camp; and not a few who have entered college."

Another soldier, James Monroe Trotter, made a similar observation. "Scattered here and there over this broad country today," he said, "are many veteran soldiers who are good readers and writers . . . who took their first lessons from some manly officer or no less manly fellow soldier . . . during such camp intervals as were allowed by . . . war."

SPEAKING OUT

African Americans looked for every opportunity to advance their education. One of their most powerful tools was the written word. Throughout the 1800s, abolitionists had published newspapers, booklets, and journals that supported emancipation. African-American soldiers used these same publications to inform the public by writing letters that described their experiences. Because they feared punishment or revenge, the black soldiers often wrote without identifying themselves. Even so, their letters brought attention to the ongoing racism they encountered.

Decades before the Civil War began, people had used the printed word to voice their objections to slavery. By 1861, black and white abolitionists had started more than 20 newspapers to speak out against slavery.

African Americans also created newspapers of their own. Writers and editors like Martin Robinson Delany, James Pennington, Charles Langston, and Henry H. Garnet (all born in slavery) used their literary skills in support of freedom. Frederick Douglass published a newspaper he called *The North Star.* African-American churches, too, created newspapers, although some lasted only a year or two. In all, African Americans ran 41 different newspapers.

The antislavery newspapers were all published locally, often with support from various antislavery societies. Such abolitionist groups worked to end slavery by informing the public, petitioning elected officials, and contributing money to African-American abolition efforts. The newspapers included speeches from antislavery leaders in government. The papers also published excerpts from slaves' life stories, parts of sermons against slavery, reports from antislavery groups, and news stories. All this information kept both blacks and whites up to date about the issues and events surrounding the fight for freedom and equality.

While the soldiers worked from within the military, African-American civilians in the North banded together to make their voices heard, as well. They already had a network of organizations that had met throughout the 1800s to promote social action, self-help, antislavery efforts, and literacy. During the war, many of these organizations turned their attention to promoting a better life for all African Americans when the war ended.

In October 1864, a gathering of 144 free African Americans from 18 states met in Syracuse, New York. This National Convention of Colored Men aimed to make clear what African Americans wanted for their future. They demanded universal abolition and legal equality. As they wrote in an address to the people of the United States,

We want the elective franchise in all the states now in the union, and the same in all such states as may come into the union hereafter. . . . The position of that right is the keystone to the arch of human liberty; and without that the whole may at any moment fall to the ground; while, with it, that liberty may stand forever.

The convention also asked that African Americans be allowed to own land from which they could create financial independence. It sought access to education for African Americans so they could share in the leadership of the United States. It also claimed the right for African Americans to worship freely in their own way.

The most urgent demand of the convention had to do with conditions for ending the war. Congress was debating the question of how to settle a peace with the South. Would peace be allowed if slavery continued, or would the South have to abolish slavery before the Union granted peace? The convention insisted that there should be no peace without abolition.

The delegates attending the Syracuse convention established a new organization called the National Equal Rights

League. This organization would be dedicated to fighting the racism that prevented African Americans from attending certain schools, holding certain jobs, and even using certain public facilities. The league would continue well beyond the time of the Civil War.

THE SPREAD OF AFRICAN-AMERICAN RIGHTS

Black soldiers continued to speak out for equal treatment in the military. So, too, did free African Americans in the North. They gathered in groups such as the National Convention of Colored Men to find ways to promote equality as citizens. The Civil War was bringing so much attention to the injustices black people in the United States had to endure that more and more people, black and white, saw the need for change. The Yearly Meeting of American Quakers sent petitions to Congress urging it to end slavery immediately everywhere. The Women's Loyal National League, a white women's group that supported the Union, sent signatures to Congress for the same purpose.

In Confederate Louisiana, free African-American men insisted that the state could not be restored to the Union when Northern troops arrived unless blacks were given the right to vote. President Lincoln wrote to Louisiana's governor, Michael Hahn, "I barely suggest for your private consideration whether some of the colored people may not be let in [to vote] . . . and especially those who have fought gallantly in our ranks."

Some of the contraband camps in the South, meanwhile, made the first baby steps toward giving new freedoms and rights to the freed slaves. Union chaplains and Northern missionaries who were responsible for supervising the camps promised that former slaves would be paid for the labor they did there and would no longer be whipped as they had been in slavery. Neither would members of their families be sold away into slavery. They would even be allowed to worship as they wished.

This wood engraving is from *The Black Phalanx,* by Joseph T. Wilson, published in 1888. It shows Confederate captives being moved through the streets of a Southern city by black Union cavalrymen.

Such issues as voting rights, wages, and even physical punishment did not top the list of concerns for the African Americans who were still living in slavery. For the families of black soldiers and contrabands, freedom from slavery remained central. They still lived in the Confederate South. They still did not know what would happen to them when the war finally ended. Congress would officially answer that question in March 1865, when it guaranteed freedom to the families of all former slaves who enlisted in the Union military. Before that could happen, however, there was a war to be fought and won.

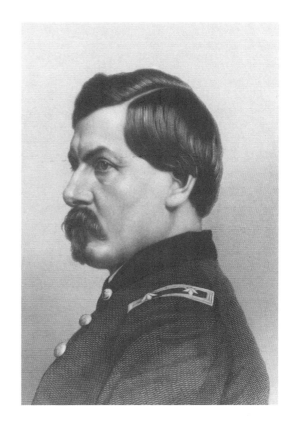

Former Union general George McClellan ran for president against Abraham Lincoln in the election of 1864. Lincoln won reelection easily.

LINCOLN'S REELECTION

As the war continued, the election neared. The Democratic Party nominated George B. McClellan as its candidate to oppose Lincoln. McClellan had been a Union general early in the war. Now he wanted the war, but not slavery, to end. The

Democrats could not have helped Lincoln more. McClellan's stand against emancipation firmly united Republicans and African Americans.

Lincoln won reelection easily. More than half of the voting population cast their ballots for him. In the Electoral College, he won 212 to 21 over McClellan. Nearly 74 percent of eligible voters took part in the election, including 154,000 soldiers who either cast absentee ballots or went home to vote. Unlike the civilians, a huge majority of the soldiers voted for Lincoln.

In 1865, President Lincoln promoted Martin R. Delany to the rank of major. Only one other African American in the Civil War, Francis E. Dumas, achieved this rank. Delany was the first African-American field officer.

At the end of 1864, eight black regiments participated in the Battle of Nashville, Tennessee. They played a vital part in defeating the Confederate army of Tennessee. Later, looking back over the year, Secretary of War Stanton would say, "The hardest fighting was done by the black troops. The forts they stormed were the worst of all."

7

The Occupation Army

This 1866 drawing shows black Union soldiers returning home from
battle to Little Rock, Arkansas. After the Civil War, the government sent
home many more white troops than black troops.

GAINS FOR BLACKS

On September 2, 1864, when General Sherman telegraphed Washington that "Atlanta is ours, and fairly won," Lincoln understood that the war's end was near. Following the president's reelection, Sherman launched what would later be known as his "March to the Sea." He moved his troops from Atlanta to Savannah, Georgia, with little opposition from the Confederates. Along the way, his army consumed or destroyed almost everything that could help the rebel army or supply the Southern people. The path of destruction he left behind was nearly 300 miles (480 km) wide.

During General William T. Sherman's "March to the Sea" in 1864, Union troops tore apart train rails in Georgia to keep the Confederate army from using the railroad system.

From the start, Sherman had refused to allow African Americans to fight in his regiments as he crossed the South. Nevertheless, the slaves he encountered along the way saw him as a savior. Poor and ragged, these newly freed people fell in behind Sherman's troops and followed them to Savannah.

By the time Sherman reached Savannah, on the coast, people knew that the South had lost the war. Union general Ulysses S. Grant was fighting Robert E. Lee's army in Virginia with success that equaled Sherman's success in Georgia. Meanwhile, Sherman needed to deal with thousands of black refugees.

On January 12, 1865, Sherman and Secretary of War Stanton met with a group of 20 black ministers and church officials from Savannah. The general wanted to know what could be done to provide for all the African Americans who had followed him to the coast. A black spokesman responded. "The way we can best take care of ourselves," he said, "is to have land . . . and till it by our labor." He explained that it would be old men, women, and children who worked the land. The young men would enlist in service to the U.S. government and earn a living wage. "We want to be placed on land," he explained, "until we are able to buy it and make it our own."

By June 1865, 40,000 freed people had settled on their new farms under the provisions of Special Field Order No. 15. Two months later, President Andrew Johnson pardoned Southern landowners and gave the land back to them. The African Americans were forced to leave.

Four days later, Sherman issued Special Field Order No. 15. In this order, he declared that the coastline and riverbanks

30 miles (48 km) inland from Charleston, South Carolina, to Jacksonville, Florida, would be reserved for settlement by freed African Americans. Each family would be allowed to claim up to 40 acres (16 ha).

Sherman next marched northward, and Southern leaders feared he would soon attack Richmond. More Confederate fighting men were desperately needed. At last, the Confederate Congress made what had earlier seemed an unthinkable decision. It voted to make Confederate soldiers out of black slaves. As spring 1865 approached, the South began to arm and train black troops. But it had waited too long. None of these troops would ever see the field of battle.

However, African-American troops in the Union army helped capture one Confederate stronghold after another all across the South. Everywhere they went, they met slaves who were suddenly free. One officer described the scene as his black regiment marched into Wilmington, North Carolina. "The frantic demonstrations of the Negro population," he said, "will never die out of my memory. Their cheers and heartfelt 'God bless ye's' and 'The chains is broke, the chains is broke,' mingled sublimely with the lusty shouts of our brave soldiery."

In Montgomery, Alabama, freed people stood all along the banks of the river that flowed through the city, cheering and singing. They danced and saluted, waving their hats and handkerchiefs at the black soldiers. When the Union forces took Richmond, the Confederate capital, some eyewitnesses would later claim that African-American troops were the first to march into the city. A white slaveholding woman described the scene: "Our . . . servants were completely crazed. They danced and shouted, men hugged each other, and women kissed. . . . Imagine the streets crowded with these people!"

Blacks across the country, in both the North and South, came out to celebrate the end of the war and a victory that would protect former slaves' newfound freedom, as shown in this illustration from a May 1866 issue of *Harper's Weekly* magazine.

THE END OF THE WAR

On April 9, 1865, General Lee surrendered his army to General Grant at Appomattox after a battle there that devastated Confederate troops. Three days later, Lee surrendered officially, handing over his weapons and the Confederate battle flags. This effectively ended the Civil War.

The Union troops who were present at the surrender responded quietly, under orders from their commanders. Confederate soldiers were Americans, after all, just like the Union soldiers. They had also fought hard and bravely. They had died by the thousands, as Union soldiers had. With the end of the war, they would no longer be "the enemy." As the Confederates marched past the Northern troops to stack their weapons, the Union men stood at attention as a sign of respect.

Among the white people of the South, there was only grief. One woman wrote, "We are scattered, stunned; the remnant of heart left alive is filled with brotherly hate." When news of the surrender reached the North, however, fireworks exploded in the sky above Washington. Throughout the Union, people cheered, celebrated, and eagerly awaited the return of their soldiers.

For African Americans everywhere, the Union victory brought great joy. African Americans had paid a steep price for their participation in the war. More than 38,000 black soldiers had lost their lives in the conflict. Their contribution played an important part in the Union victory. Because of that victory, they could finally look forward to the total abolition of slavery. After nearly 250 years, people in the United States would no longer be allowed to own other human beings as property.

Just five days after the South surrendered, the joy of the victors turned to horror. On April 14, 1865, an actor named John Wilkes Booth shot and killed President Abraham Lincoln. Booth, a racist Confederate sympathizer, hated Lincoln's plans to reunite North and South under a policy of emancipation. African Americans reacted with deep sorrow to this act of violence. As one black soldier put it, "Humanity has lost a firm advocate, our race its Patron Saint." Another soldier wrote to his sister, "I cannot paint to you the grief and indignation that our officers feel. With us of the U.S. Colored Army the death of Lincoln is indeed the loss of a friend. From him we received our commission—and toward him we have even looked as toward a Father."

Some black soldiers believed that Lincoln's most important work had been completed. "He has done the work given him," one man wrote. The men expected that their future would be bright. Unfortunately, their hopes would soon be disappointed.

The Thirteenth Amendment

Even before the Civil War ended, Congress approved a change to the U.S. Constitution, called an amendment, that would end slavery for good throughout the country. No longer could some states abolish slavery while others kept it legal. The Thirteenth Amendment has two parts, or sections. One outlaws slavery throughout the entire nation. The other gives the government the right to enforce the law. The amendment reads:

Section 1. Neither slavery nor involuntary servitude, except as a punishment for crime whereof the party shall have been duly convicted, shall exist within the United States, or any place subject to their jurisdiction.

Section 2. Congress shall have the power to enforce this article by appropriate legislation.

The amendment was approved by the states in December 1865.

BLACK TROOPS AFTER THE WAR

With the war over, there was no longer a need for the government to support the 1 million men still in service to the army. Such support cost more than the government could afford, and families wanted their soldiers to come home. Congress and the new president, Andrew Johnson—who had been Lincoln's vice president—acted quickly to downsize the armed forces.

Work remained for the armed forces, however. The nation needed to be put back together. Laws concerning how the South would reenter the Union had to be enforced. The 4 million slaves who were freed by the war required help making the transition to freedom. This process came to be known as Reconstruction.

The government now had to decide which soldiers would be "mustered out" (allowed to go home) and which would continue to serve. It chose to send home a much higher percentage of white soldiers than black. The government believed that keeping a higher percentage of African Americans in uniform would give those who had been slaves a way to support themselves. It also saw the political advantage of sending home the soldiers who could show their appreciation with their votes.

The black soldiers soon discovered that the postwar life of an African American in uniform was difficult. Slavery had ended. Racism had not. White citizens in both the North and South objected to the presence of black soldiers among them. One army officer wrote, "New Englanders have always peculiarly loved the Negro, but they do not love him in their midst; they prefer him away in Georgia or Louisiana, whither they can send him their sympathy by mail."

This engraving from 1864 shows black Union troops freeing slaves in North Carolina near the end of the war. Southerners did not easily accept black soldiers in their midst after the war.

People in the South, of course, were outraged at the sight of former slaves given the power to move freely among them. Even worse, some black soldiers had the job of seeing that laws protecting freed people were obeyed. Many Southerners reacted with extreme disrespect, and sometimes with violence, against the African Americans.

Some whites mocked the black soldiers, trying to start fights that would get the black soldiers into trouble, or accused the black troops of stealing or encouraging freed people to make trouble against whites. In a Louisiana tavern, violence erupted between white customers and African-American soldiers. In Virginia, a white person living near the camp of black troops tried to poison the camp's well water. In South Carolina, locals tried to wipe out an entire black regiment by sabotaging the train in which they were being transported. In Texas, a local paper reported that white people "with blackened faces and in the Uniform of United States Soldiers," committed crimes against other whites "to get an order issued for the removal of the only reliable [black] troops."

Crimes and mockery against the African-American soldiers sometimes led to murder. In numerous instances, white civilians found ways to isolate one or a few black soldiers and kill them. When the most hateful whites failed to hurt the soldiers, they often attacked their families, stealing from them, forcing them out of their homes, or physically attacking them. In some cases, white U.S. soldiers abused black servicemen.

Too often, the military failed to address these problems. If African-American troops fought back, their commanders punished them while the whites walked away free. The officers had to keep the troops under control. They could not let the blacks take revenge. The injustice of what the black soldiers faced gave them a taste of what would come throughout Reconstruction and beyond.

RECONSTRUCTION DUTY

The postwar picture was not entirely bleak for black soldiers. Six weeks before Lincoln was assassinated, the government had established the Freedmen's Bureau. This agency helped former slaves in the South find family members who had been sold away or moved during the war. It watched over the interests of blacks, working to ensure justice for them in the courts and negotiating fair contracts for their labor and property. The bureau also aided efforts to establish black churches and schools. African-American troops were assigned to enforce the orders of this agency.

Army School

Most white officers in the U.S. Colored Troops believed that education for their black soldiers was a must. Army chaplains and a few officers usually headed the programs, along with some hired civilian teachers. Officers' families and benevolent societies (groups organized for helping people in need) in the North donated books, blackboards, and other necessary materials.

At first, officers needed to teach the soldiers the reading and writing they had been denied in civilian life. (Many of the black soldiers came from slave states in which it had been illegal to teach an African American to read.) Once the men mastered these basics, they could move on to arithmetic, geography, history, Bible study, and even military tactics. Nearly every black regiment made education a part of its daily schedule.

One company commander later reported that before their education began, only four or five of his men "could read a little." Six weeks into their training, all of his troops knew the alphabet and many had learned to read. The men themselves developed a sense of pride that would help them face the battle for full equality ahead.

Not only did African-American soldiers have this opportunity to help other Southern blacks in the aftermath of slavery, but they also had time to help themselves. Just as during the war, military service included enough free time for the men to further their own education. The Freedmen's Bureau supported the work of Northern teachers who traveled south to teach freed people. In addition, the officers of black troops supported programs of education and religious study. They believed that such programs would not only prepare the men for a life of freedom after Reconstruction, but also keep them from seeking revenge for the years of slavery and prejudice they had suffered.

This wood engraving from an 1866 U.S. newspaper shows a settlement of freed blacks in Trent River, North Carolina, the year after the end of the war.

Even so, most of the worst assignments during Reconstruction went to the black troops. They were often the ones sent to remove the bodies of dead soldiers from major battlefields so the remains could be buried properly. The army sent black units to locations where diseases such as malaria were common while decent medical care and adequate provisions were lacking. The troops endured terrible living conditions and rarely received their due wages.

In one extreme case, more than half of an entire black regiment in Texas suffered from scurvy, a disease caused by a lack of vitamin C. They needed the kinds of fresh vegetables and fruits that would provide the vitamin, but none were sent. An army hospital that could hold 80 patients was flooded with more than 500 men, and these were only the sickest. Many others suffered without any medical attention or relief from duty.

AFRICAN-AMERICAN TROOPS FIGHT BACK

Eventually, some of the black soldiers stood up against the hardships and injustices they had to face. Some troops rebelled, especially when it was their own officers who made them suffer. To keep troops under control, officers sometimes used unusually harsh punishments. They might tie black soldiers up by their thumbs, gag them, or close them into a small box under a burning sun for hours on end.

Such treatment roused the troops to mutiny. "These officers think they can do just as they have a mind to with us now

After escaping slavery in 1862, Susie King Taylor served in a black regiment of the Union army as a laundress and a teacher. Forty years later, in 1902, racism continued. Looking back on that war, she wrote this:

My dear friends! Do we know or think of that war of '61? . . . We do not, as the black race, properly appreciate the old veterans, white or black, as we ought to. I know what they went through, especially those black men, for the Confederates had no mercy on them. . . . I was the wife of one of those men who did not get a penny for eighteen months for their services. . . .

All we ask for is "equal justice," the same that is accorded to all other races who come to this country . . . we are denied what is rightfully our own in a country which the labor of our forefathers helped to make what it is.

the war is over," said one soldier, "but we will show them, if we have to kill every one of them!" The angry troops did not actually kill their officers, although some black regiments did rise up against harsh leaders. Dozens of African-American soldiers were court-martialed for mutiny.

Many more chose more traditional means of protest. They had fought hard for their freedom, and they did not intend to lose it now. Black servicemen believed that they had more than earned equality. They made their voices heard in every way they could. They complained to their commanders and wrote letters to government leaders in Washington and to newspaper editors. As Sergeant Henry Maxwell stated after the war, "We want two more boxes besides the cartridge box [which held ammunition for a gun], the ballot and the jury box." It was not enough that African Americans had won the right to fight alongside their white fellows. Now they wanted the right to vote, the right to serve on a jury, and all the rights of citizenship.

CARRYING THE FIGHT FORWARD

The Civil War brought the most important change in the lives of African Americans. It ended slavery and gave African Americans an essential chance to prove their courage and abilities. In February 1865, an editor for *The Christian Recorder* wrote,

> *When we reflect upon the condition . . . of the African race, at the present, contrasted with that . . . of a world four years ago, well may we boast . . . an admission of our valor, our manhood, our courage, has been made by our former oppressors; partial equality has been extended to us, and our rights as citizens have been recognized, in a great measure. . . . The white soldiers of our army find us an indispensable acquisition to their numbers, and fear not to fight upon the same ground with us.*

The war did not solve the problem of racism. Nor did it give African Americans the full rights of citizenship that should have been theirs from the start. The fight for real freedom would go on. The battle for color-blind equality continues to the present day.

Time Line

1860

November 6   Abraham Lincoln is elected the 16th president of the United States.

1861

April 12   Confederate forces fire on Fort Sumter, South Carolina.

May 24   General Benjamin F. Butler declares fugitive slaves "contrabands" of war.

August 6   The First Confiscation Act takes away slaveholders' right to reclaim fugitive slaves formerly used in the Confederate war effort.

1862

March 13   Congress forbids the U.S. Army and Navy to return fugitive slaves to their owners.

May 9   General David Hunter issues his own emancipation proclamation and soon after organizes the First South Carolina Colored Regiment.

July 17   The Second Confiscation Act frees slaves in states that are in rebellion and authorizes the president to employ "persons of African descent" in any way needed to suppress the rebellion. The Militia Act provides for the military employment of African Americans, granting them freedom.

October 27–28   The First Kansas Colored Volunteer Regiment engages Confederates at Island Mound, Missouri.

| December 23 | Confederate president Jefferson Davis proclaims that black Union soldiers and their officers are not to be given the rights of prisoners of war. |

1863

January 1	President Lincoln issues the Emancipation Proclamation.
January 26	The First South Carolina Volunteer Regiment (African Descent) engages Confederates at Township, Florida, shortly after being mustered at Beaufort, South Carolina.
March 26	The secretary of war issues an order directing the organization of black regiments in the Mississippi Valley.
March 30	The 54th Massachusetts Volunteer Regiment is mustered in to serve with the Union army.
May 22	The Bureau of Colored Troops is created within the War Department.
May 27	The U.S. Colored Troops prove their bravery in battle at Fort Hudson on the Mississippi River.
June 7	The battle at Milliken's Bend, Louisiana, includes 1,250 contrabands recently mustered in as the Ninth and 11th Louisiana and First Mississippi Colored Volunteer Regiments.
July 17	The First Kansas Colored Volunteer Regiment fights in the Battle of Honey Springs, in present-day Oklahoma.
July 18	The 54th Massachusetts Regiment leads the assault on Fort Wagner, South Carolina.
July 30	President Lincoln threatens retaliation for Confederate mistreatment of black prisoners of war.

1864

| February 20 | The Battle of Olustee, Florida, includes the 54th Massachusetts and the Eighth and 35th U.S. Colored Infantry Regiments. |

April 8	The Senate approves the Thirteenth Amendment to the U.S. Constitution, abolishing slavery.
April 12	Black and white Union troops are slaughtered by Confederates at Fort Pillow, Tennessee.
June 15	Congress makes pay for black soldiers equal to that of white soldiers—retroactive to January 1, 1864, for former slaves, and retroactive to time of enlistment for free blacks.
September 29	The Battle of Chaffin's Farm, Virginia, includes 12 U.S. black infantry regiments and one cavalry regiment.
November 8	Lincoln is reelected president.
November 30	The Battle of Honey Hill, South Carolina, includes the 54th and 55th Massachusetts, and the 32nd, 35th, and 102nd U.S. Colored Infantry Regiments.
December 3	The 25th Army Corps is organized—the only army corps made up of all-black infantry regiments.

1865

March 3	Congress establishes the Bureau of Refugees, Freedmen, and Abandoned Lands (Freedmen's Bureau) to oversee the transition from slavery to freedom.
March 13	The Confederate Congress approves the recruitment of black soldiers.
March 31–April 9	The Battle of Fort Blakely, Alabama, includes 11 black infantry regiments.
April 9	Robert E. Lee surrenders the Confederate army at Appomattox Courthouse in Virginia, ending the Civil War.
April 14	President Lincoln is assassinated. Vice President Andrew Johnson becomes the 17th president of the United States.
December 18	The Thirteenth Amendment to the U.S. Constitution is enacted, abolishing slavery throughout the United States.

Glossary

abolitionist   A person who seeks an immediate end to slavery.

civil rights   The rights of personal liberty guaranteed by the U.S. Constitution.

contraband   Fugitive slaves who came under the control of Union troops during the Civil War.

Deep South   Usually refers to the part of the United States that includes Alabama, Arkansas, Florida, Georgia, Louisiana, Mississippi, Texas, and parts of the Carolinas and Tennessee.

emancipation   The act of freeing slaves.

Freedmen's Bureau   An organization that assisted the newly freed African Americans after the Civil War.

fugitive   A person who escapes from slave owners or law officials.

plantation   A large farm that relied on slaves to produce one main crop.

prejudice   An unreasonable bias against or intolerance of others.

racism   Prejudice based on race.

Reconstruction   A federal program after the Civil War to readmit Southern states into the Union and provide equal rights for African Americans.

refugees   People forced out of their homes because of war or a natural disaster.

secede   To break away from a larger group or government and become independent.

segregation   Separating whites and blacks and requiring them to use different public facilities, such as parks and schools.

spiritual   A folk hymn of a type developed by blacks in the American South that combined African and European elements and expressed deep emotion.

suffrage   The right to vote.

Thirteenth Amendment   An amendment to the U.S. Constitution prohibiting slavery.

watch night service   A religious service lasting until after midnight, especially on New Year's Eve.

Further Reading

BOOKS

Cox, Clinton. *Undying Glory: The Story of the Massachusetts Fifty-Fourth Regiment.* New York: Scholastic, 1993.

Hansen, Joyce. *Between Two Fires: Black Soldiers in the Civil War.* New York: Franklin Watts, 1993.

Haskins, Jim. *Black Stars of Civil War Times.* New York: John Wiley, 2003.

Herbert, Janis. *The Civil War for Kids: A History with 21 Activities.* Chicago: Chicago Review Press, 1999.

McPherson, James M. *Marching Toward Freedom: Blacks in the Civil War, 1861–1865.* New York: Facts On File, 1991.

Stowe, Harriet Beecher. *Uncle Tom's Cabin.* New York: Penguin Classics, 1981.

WEB SITES

African American Civil War Memorial Freedom Foundation Museum & Visitors Center. "African American Civil War Memorial." URL: http://www.afroamcivilwar.org/. Downloaded on July 6, 2005.

Library of Congress. "African American Odyssey: The Civil War." URL: http://memory. loc.gov/ammem/aaohtml/exhibit/aopart4.html. Downloaded on July 6, 2005.

Public Broadcasting Service (PBS). "Africans in America: Part 4, The Civil War." URL: http://www.pbs.org/wgbh/aia/part4/4narr5.html. Downloaded on July 6, 2005.

Smithsonian Institution. "CivilWar@Smithsonian: Soldiering." URL: http://civilwar.si.edu/soldiering_intro.html. Downloaded on July 6, 2005.

Index